Emerging Paradigms of the Indian Print Industry

Research Insights and Emerging Technologies

Dr. Mohit Kumar, Rekha Rani

ink Scribe

Paradigms of the Indian Print Industry

Publisher: Inkscribe Publishing Pvt. Ltd.
ISBN Number: 978-1-966421-81-8

Table of Contents

Preface

The printing industry has undergone a remarkable transformation over the past few decades, driven by technological advancements, evolving market demands, and the integration of digital and automated solutions. India, as one of the fastest-growing printing markets in the world, stands at a crucial juncture where traditional printing methods are gradually giving way to innovative and sustainable alternatives. This book, *Emerging Paradigms of the Indian Print Industry: Research Insights and Emerging Technologies*, delves into the theoretical, methodological, and practical aspects of this transformation, providing a comprehensive perspective on the future of printing.

Designed primarily for academicians, researchers, and students in printing technology and media studies, this book aims to bridge the gap between conventional printing practices and modern technological interventions. By examining global trends, the rise of digital printing, AI-driven automation, sustainable printing practices, and ethical considerations, we provide an in-depth analysis of the industry's evolution and its future trajectory.

A key focus of this book is on research methodologies and forecasting techniques that help predict industry shifts. With the increasing dominance of digital printing, smart packaging, printed electronics, and 3D printing, understanding the implications of these advancements is crucial for both academic research and industrial practice. Moreover, the book highlights India's unique market dynamics—its rapid adoption of digital technologies, challenges in sustainability, and the growing role of automation in print production.

As we navigate this era of rapid technological change, this book serves as a guide to understanding the factors shaping the future of printing in India and the global context. By presenting a balanced view of opportunities and challenges, it encourages further research and discussion on how the industry can adapt, innovate, and thrive in an increasingly digital and eco-conscious world.

We hope this book inspires researchers, students, and industry professionals to explore new avenues of study and contribute to the ongoing transformation of the printing industry.

Dr. Mohit Kumar
&
Rekha Rani

Introduction to Printing Technology

1.1 Evolution of Printing from Traditional to Modern Techniques

Printing has undergone significant transformations since its inception. From ancient civilizations using simple methods of imprinting images onto clay, textiles, and other materials to the sophisticated digital and 3D printing technologies of today, the journey of printing reflects humanity's continuous quest for innovation and knowledge dissemination.

One of the earliest recorded printing methods was woodblock printing, which originated in China around the 7th century CE. This technique involved carving entire pages of text or images onto wooden blocks, applying ink, and then pressing them onto paper or fabric. While effective, this method was labour-intensive and limited in its ability to reproduce large volumes quickly. The Chinese also pioneered early forms of movable type printing during the Song Dynasty (11th century), which involved creating individual characters on clay or metal blocks that could be rearranged to form different texts. However, due to the complexity of the Chinese writing system, this method did not gain widespread popularity in China.

In the 15th century, Johannes Gutenberg of Germany revolutionized printing with the invention of the movable type printing press. Unlike earlier attempts, Gutenberg's system used metal type pieces that were durable and could be reused. His printing press enabled mass production of books, making literature and knowledge more accessible to a broader audience. The first major book printed using his press, the Gutenberg Bible (1455), demonstrated the potential of the new technology. The press played a key role in advancing literacy, education, and the spread of information throughout Europe, sparking movements such as the Renaissance and the Protestant Reformation.

With the growth of literacy and demand for printed materials, further innovations emerged. By the 19th century, the printing industry was transformed by the Industrial Revolution, which introduced mechanized presses capable of producing thousands of copies in a single day. Steam-powered printing presses significantly increased efficiency, enabling mass production of newspapers, books, and pamphlets at lower costs. The rotary press, developed in the mid-19th century, further improved speed by using continuous rolls of paper rather than individual sheets. This period marked the golden age of print media, with newspapers becoming widely available and influencing public opinion on a global scale.

By the late 19th and early 20th centuries, offset printing, flexography, and gravure printing emerged, significantly enhancing efficiency and print quality. Offset printing, developed in the early 20th century, became the dominant method for producing newspapers, books, and marketing materials due to its superior image reproduction and cost-effectiveness. Flexography, primarily used for packaging and labeling, allowed for printing on a variety of non-porous surfaces such as plastics and foils. Gravure printing, known for its high image quality and durability, became popular for magazine and packaging printing, making it one of the preferred choices for large-scale production.

The advent of computers in the late 20th century introduced digital printing and computer-to-plate (CTP) technology, revolutionizing the industry by improving speed, customization, and sustainability. Digital printing eliminated the need for traditional printing plates, enabling short-run production and personalized printing solutions. Inkjet and laser printing technologies allowed for direct printing from digital files, reducing setup costs and making printing accessible to smaller businesses and individuals. The rise of desktop publishing software further democratized print production, allowing designers and publishers to create high-quality materials without relying on traditional printing houses.

As digital printing gained popularity, traditional printing methods adapted to remain competitive. Hybrid printing systems, which combine digital and offset technologies, emerged to provide greater flexibility and efficiency. For example, digital enhancements such as variable data printing (VDP) allowed businesses to personalize marketing materials with unique customer information, making direct mail campaigns more effective.

In recent years, 3D printing has further expanded the definition of printing, allowing for the creation of physical objects from digital models. Unlike traditional 2D printing, 3D printing builds objects layer by layer using materials such as plastic, metal, and even biological tissues. This technology has revolutionized industries ranging from manufacturing to medicine, enabling rapid prototyping, custom prosthetics, and even organ printing. The ability to create complex structures with minimal waste has made 3D printing an essential tool in modern engineering and design.

Today, the printing industry continues to evolve with advancements in artificial intelligence, automation, and eco-friendly materials, ensuring that print remains a vital part of communication and manufacturing. AI-driven printing systems can optimize production workflows, predict maintenance needs, and enhance image quality. Automation in printing plants has reduced human intervention, increasing efficiency and reducing errors. Additionally, sustainable printing practices, such as the use of vegetable-based inks, recycled paper, and energy-efficient machinery, are helping the industry reduce its environmental footprint.

Looking ahead, the future of printing will likely see further integration with digital technologies. Augmented reality (AR) and smart packaging are emerging trends that blend print with digital interactivity. AR-enabled printed materials allow users to scan images with their smartphones to access videos, animations, and other digital content. Smart packaging uses printed sensors and QR codes to provide real-time product information and track supply chains.

Despite the dominance of digital media, printing continues to play a critical role in education, publishing, marketing, and manufacturing. The ability to physically interact with printed materials provides a unique sensory experience that digital screens cannot replicate. As printing technologies continue to evolve, the industry will remain an essential force in shaping communication and innovation worldwide.

1.2 Importance of Printing in Knowledge Dissemination

Printing has been crucial in shaping societies by facilitating education, communication, and cultural exchange. Before the invention of the printing press, knowledge was preserved through handwritten manuscripts, limiting access to information. The painstaking process of copying texts by hand made books rare and expensive, restricting knowledge to a privileged few. As a result, only the elite, including clergy and scholars, had access to significant texts, leaving the majority of the population without the ability to acquire knowledge freely.

The invention of Gutenberg's printing press in the 15th century revolutionized the way information was shared, making books widely available and fostering literacy and intellectual growth. This mass production of printed materials democratized knowledge, enabling people from all walks of life to learn, share ideas, and challenge existing beliefs.

The spread of printed texts played a key role in the Renaissance, a cultural rebirth that emphasized humanism, art, and science. The Reformation, which saw the rise of Protestantism, was significantly fueled by the accessibility of religious texts and pamphlets. Similarly, the Industrial Revolution was aided by printed instructional materials, technical manuals, and educational resources that empowered workers with new skills.

Printing has had a profound impact on communication and mass media. The newspaper industry, in particular, thrived due to advancements in printing technology, allowing for the rapid spread of news and ideas. By the 17th century, newspapers and printed pamphlets were instrumental in informing the public about politics, economic affairs, and social issues. This development enhanced civic engagement, encouraged public discourse, and contributed to the formation of democratic societies. Even today, print journalism continues to be a critical component of media, with newspapers, magazines, and newsletters providing in-depth reporting and analysis.

Beyond news and information, printing has been essential in shaping cultural identities. Books, religious scriptures, and literary works have contributed to the preservation and dissemination of languages, traditions, and philosophies across generations. The ability to record histories, folklore, and literature in written form has ensured that diverse cultures maintain their heritage. Additionally, printed music notation allowed for the widespread sharing of compositions, fostering musical innovation and appreciation worldwide.

In education, printing has played an irreplaceable role in making knowledge accessible to students and researchers. The production of textbooks, reference materials, and scientific papers has allowed for the standardization of education systems across countries. Educational institutions rely heavily on printed resources to structure curricula and facilitate learning. The impact of print extends beyond traditional schools, as adult literacy programs and distance learning initiatives benefit from printed study materials. Academic journals, conference proceedings, and research publications remain the backbone of scholarly communication, enabling scientists and experts to share findings, collaborate, and advance their respective fields.

Even with the rise of digital technologies, printed books and educational materials continue to be widely used due to their durability, ease of use, and lack of dependency on electricity or internet connectivity. Many studies suggest that reading from printed materials improves comprehension, retention, and focus compared to digital screens. Additionally, print allows for annotation and note-taking, which are crucial for students and professionals engaged in intensive research and study.

Printing is also indispensable for government operations, legal systems, and healthcare. Official records, legislative documents, and constitutional texts are traditionally printed to maintain legal authenticity and prevent tampering. Laws, policies, and regulations are disseminated through printed bulletins and legal notices, ensuring transparency and public access. In the medical field, printed literature—including textbooks, journals, patient records, and drug labels—plays a vital role in healthcare education, research, and practice. The pharmaceutical industry, in particular, relies on printed packaging inserts and labels to communicate critical information about medications, dosages, and safety guidelines.

Another essential function of print is its role in preserving historical and archival materials. Libraries and national archives store centuries' worth of printed documents that serve as valuable resources for researchers, historians, and policymakers. Unlike digital data, which is susceptible to hacking, data corruption, and technological obsolescence, printed records have proven to withstand the test of time. Many historical texts and manuscripts that were printed hundreds of years ago remain accessible today, while digital records from just a few decades ago face issues related to format compatibility and data loss. As a result, print remains a reliable medium for long-term knowledge preservation.

Despite digital alternatives, print media remains a trusted and tangible source of information, reinforcing its relevance in modern society. Printed books, newspapers, and magazines continue to hold an inherent credibility that digital media sometimes lacks, particularly in an era of misinformation and fake news. Studies show that printed advertisements and marketing materials also leave a lasting impression on consumers compared to digital ads, demonstrating the unique psychological impact of physical print.

Furthermore, print has expanded beyond traditional uses, evolving into innovative fields such as augmented reality (AR) printing, interactive packaging, and smart labels. AR-enhanced books and printed materials allow users to scan pages with smartphones to access additional digital content, creating an immersive learning experience. Smart labels on food packaging provide consumers with instant access to product information, sustainability credentials, and traceability details. These advancements showcase how print continues to adapt and integrate with new technologies to enhance knowledge dissemination in modern times.

Looking ahead, the significance of printing in knowledge dissemination will continue to evolve alongside technological advancements. While digital platforms provide instant access to vast amounts of information, print offers permanence, credibility, and sensory engagement that digital formats cannot fully replicate. The future of printing will likely see a hybrid approach, where print and digital mediums complement each other to maximize knowledge accessibility and retention.

In conclusion, the impact of printing on knowledge dissemination is undeniable. From its historical role in education, culture, and governance to its continued relevance in an increasingly digital world, print remains a powerful tool for preserving and sharing information. As the printing industry continues to innovate and adapt, it will remain an essential force in shaping human knowledge and communication.

1.3 Overview of Major Printing Processes

Printing encompasses various techniques, each suited for different applications. Over the years, different printing methods have been developed to cater to specific needs in commercial, industrial, and artistic fields. These methods vary in terms of quality, speed, cost, and suitability for different substrates. Below is an in-depth exploration of the major printing processes:

1.3.1 Letterpress Printing

One of the oldest printing methods, letterpress printing uses raised type to transfer ink onto paper. This technique was widely used for book and newspaper printing for centuries before being largely replaced by offset printing. Today, letterpress printing is primarily used for artistic and specialty applications, such as wedding invitations, business cards, and limited-edition prints. It provides a unique tactile feel with deep impressions, which makes it popular for high-end design projects.

Advantages:

- Produces high-quality, durable prints
- Creates a distinctive embossed effect on paper
- Ideal for limited-edition or specialty printing

Disadvantages:

- Time-consuming and labor-intensive
- Not suitable for high-speed, mass production

1.3.2 Offset Printing

Offset printing is the most widely used commercial printing method today. It works on the principle of transferring an inked image from a plate to a rubber blanket and then onto the printing surface. This indirect process ensures high-quality image reproduction with excellent color accuracy.

Applications:

- Newspapers, books, and magazines
- Marketing materials such as brochures and flyers
- Packaging and labels

Advantages:

- Cost-effective for large print runs
- Consistently high image quality
- Works on a variety of paper types

Disadvantages:

- High initial setup cost
- Not ideal for short-run printing

1.3.3 Flexographic Printing

Flexographic printing, commonly known as flexo printing, is widely used in the packaging industry. It uses flexible rubber or polymer plates that can print on a variety of materials, including plastic, foil, and cardboard. It is ideal for printing large volumes of labels, packaging materials, and flexible wraps.

Applications:

- Food packaging and beverage labels
- Plastic bags and cartons
- Wrapping papers and wallpapers

Advantages:

- Fast printing process suitable for high-volume production
- Can print on non-porous surfaces
- Uses quick-drying inks, reducing production time

Disadvantages:

- Initial setup can be expensive
- Lower image resolution compared to offset printing

1.3.4 Gravure Printing

Gravure printing is best suited for high-volume production, such as magazines, wallpapers, and flexible packaging materials. It uses engraved cylinders to transfer ink onto the substrate, making it ideal for printing fine details and continuous-tone images.

Applications:

- High-end magazines and catalogs
- Decorative wallpapers and laminates
- Packaging materials

Advantages:

- Produces high-quality prints with excellent detail
- Durable printing plates that last for long print runs
- Works well with continuous-tone images

Disadvantages:

- High setup costs due to the need for engraved cylinders
- Not cost-effective for small-scale production

1.3.5 Screen Printing

Screen printing is a versatile method that can print on various surfaces, including fabric, plastic, metal, and glass. It uses a mesh screen and a stencil to transfer ink onto the substrate. This technique is widely used for signage, apparel printing, and promotional materials.

Applications:

- T-shirts, fabric, and textiles
- Billboards, posters, and signage
- Customized merchandise such as mugs and bags

Advantages:

- Works on a variety of materials
- Long-lasting and durable prints
- Can create vibrant and opaque colors

Disadvantages:

- Not ideal for fine details or photographic prints
- Labor-intensive and slow for large-scale production

1.3.6 Digital Printing

Digital printing includes inkjet and laser printing, enabling quick, cost-effective, and customizable printing solutions. Unlike traditional methods, digital printing does not require printing plates, making it ideal for short-run jobs, personalized prints, and variable data printing.

Applications:

- Personalized marketing materials
- Business cards, brochures, and posters
- Short-run book publishing

Advantages:

- No setup costs; ideal for small batches
- Quick turnaround time
- Allows for customization and on-demand printing

Disadvantages:

- Higher cost per unit compared to offset for large volumes
- Limited in terms of specialty inks and substrates

1.3.7 3D Printing

3D printing is a revolutionary technique that builds three-dimensional objects layer by layer using digital models. This process, also known as additive manufacturing, is used in industries ranging from healthcare to aerospace and architecture.

Applications:

- Medical prosthetics and implants
- Automotive and aerospace components
- Architectural models and prototypes

Advantages:

- Enables rapid prototyping and customization
- Reduces material waste
- Allows for the creation of complex geometries

Disadvantages:

- Slower production time compared to traditional manufacturing
- Limited material options compared to conventional manufacturing methods

1.3.8 The Evolution of Printing Methods

Each printing method has evolved to meet the demands of its respective industries, allowing businesses to optimize cost, efficiency, and quality. While traditional printing techniques such as letterpress and offset remain relevant, the rise of digital and 3D printing has introduced new possibilities for customization and rapid production. The printing industry continues to innovate, integrating artificial intelligence, automation, and sustainable practices to adapt to changing consumer needs and environmental concerns.

Looking ahead, advancements in smart printing, augmented reality, and nanotechnology-based printing could further revolutionize how we produce and interact with printed materials. The combination of traditional and digital printing methods will continue to shape the future of communication, manufacturing, and artistic expression.

1.4.1 Impact of Digital Media on Print

The rise of digital alternatives, including e-books, online newspapers, and digital advertising, has significantly impacted traditional print media. Newspaper and magazine circulation has declined in many regions, as consumers increasingly turn to online news sources and digital reading platforms. However, rather than making print obsolete, digital advancements have pushed the industry to evolve. Many publishers now offer both print and digital editions, ensuring accessibility while catering to different consumer preferences. For example, newspapers such as *The New York Times* and *The Guardian* maintain strong print editions while expanding their digital presence to reach global audiences.

1.4.2 The Hybrid Publishing Model

Hybrid publishing models combine print and digital content, offering consumers a choice between traditional and digital reading experiences. Books, magazines, and newspapers increasingly feature QR codes, augmented reality (AR) elements, and interactive features that connect physical print to digital content. Educational publishers, for example, integrate print textbooks with online resources, allowing students to access multimedia materials such as videos, quizzes, and additional learning modules.

1.4.3 Innovations in Print Technology

Modern printing innovations have enabled seamless integration with digital technologies, enhancing user experience and creating new marketing opportunities. Some key advancements include:

- **Augmented Reality (AR) in Print:** AR technology allows printed materials to come alive with digital content. By scanning a printed page with a smartphone or tablet, users can view interactive videos, animations, or 3D models. This technology is being used in books, magazines, and advertising campaigns to engage audiences in new ways.
- **Interactive Packaging and Smart Labels:** Many industries, particularly in food, pharmaceuticals, and consumer goods, use smart labels that contain QR codes, near-field communication (NFC) chips, or embedded sensors. These labels provide real-time product information, authenticity verification, and even expiration date tracking.
- **Personalized and Variable Data Printing:** Digital printing enables brands to produce customized marketing materials, such as personalized direct mail, business cards, and brochures, tailored to individual consumers. This enhances engagement and increases the effectiveness of printed advertisements.

1.4.4 Sustainability and Eco-Friendly Printing Practices

As environmental concerns grow, the printing industry is adopting sustainable practices to reduce its carbon footprint. These include:

- **Vegetable-based inks:** Traditional petroleum-based inks contain harmful chemicals. Vegetable-based inks, derived from renewable sources such as soy, reduce environmental impact while maintaining high print quality.
- **Recycled and FSC-certified paper:** Many print manufacturers now use paper certified by the Forest Stewardship Council (FSC) or incorporate recycled materials to promote sustainable forestry practices.
- **Waterless printing:** Traditional offset printing requires significant amounts of water and chemicals for plate cleaning. Waterless

printing eliminates these wasteful processes, reducing pollution and chemical usage.

- **Energy-efficient production:** Printing companies are integrating renewable energy sources, such as solar and wind power, into their production processes to lower energy consumption and greenhouse gas emissions.

1.4.5 The Continued Relevance of Print in a Digital World

While digital media continues to grow, printing retains its significance in packaging, advertising, and specialized publishing sectors. Certain industries and consumer preferences ensure that print remains indispensable:

- **Packaging Industry:** The demand for high-quality printed labels, packaging, and branding materials remains strong, as companies rely on visually appealing designs to attract consumers. Flexible packaging, folding cartons, and corrugated packaging all utilize advanced printing technologies to enhance shelf appeal.
- **Tactile Experience and Trust:** Research suggests that printed materials create a stronger emotional connection with readers than digital content. Studies have shown that people retain more information when reading from print compared to digital screens. Additionally, print is often perceived as more credible than digital sources, particularly in journalism and advertising.
- **Printed Advertising:** Despite the rise of digital marketing, print advertising—such as direct mail, brochures, and outdoor billboards—continues to be an effective marketing tool. Many brands combine print and digital strategies to maximize audience reach and engagement.
- **Security Printing:** Important documents, such as banknotes, passports, government IDs, and official certificates, still rely on

print due to security concerns. Advanced security features, such as holograms, UV inks, and microprinting, help prevent counterfeiting and fraud.

1.4.6 The Future of Printing in the Digital Age

Printing's ability to evolve with technological advancements ensures that it will remain relevant in both traditional and emerging markets. The integration of artificial intelligence (AI) and automation is further transforming the industry, improving efficiency and quality control. Some emerging trends include:

- **AI-powered Print Optimization:** AI-driven software can analyze data to improve print quality, reduce waste, and predict maintenance needs for printing equipment.
- **On-Demand and Cloud Printing:** Cloud-based printing solutions enable users to print remotely, reducing the need for large-scale printing infrastructure.
- **Nongraphic Printing:** A next-generation printing technology that enhances ink efficiency and print resolution while minimizing waste.
- **Biodegradable and Smart Packaging:** The development of biodegradable inks and materials for eco-friendly packaging solutions aligns with global sustainability goals.

While digital innovations continue to reshape the industry, the fundamental role of printing remains intact. As automation and artificial intelligence continue to shape the future of printing, the industry will continue integrating new technologies to enhance efficiency, reduce environmental impact, and create new possibilities for print communication.

Literature Review and Historical Evolution

2.1 Early History and Development of Printing

The history of printing dates back to ancient civilizations, where humans sought ways to reproduce texts and images efficiently. The earliest known printing methods can be traced to Mesopotamian civilizations around 3000 BCE, where cylinder seals were used to roll impressions onto clay tablets. These early forms of printing played a crucial role in record-keeping and administration. Similarly, ancient Egyptians used carved stamps to imprint symbols onto papyrus scrolls.

A major breakthrough in early printing was **woodblock printing**, developed in China during the Tang Dynasty (618-907 CE). This technique involved carving entire pages of text or illustrations onto wooden blocks, applying ink, and pressing them onto paper or cloth. The earliest known example of woodblock printing is the **Diamond Sutra**, a Buddhist scripture printed in 868 CE. While effective, this method was labor-intensive, requiring a new block to be carved for each page, making mass production difficult.

The next significant advancement came with the invention of **movable type printing** by Bi Sheng in China around 1040 CE during the Song Dynasty. Unlike woodblock printing, movable type allowed individual characters to be rearranged, making the printing process more flexible and efficient. Bi Sheng used clay-based characters, which were later improved upon by

Korean and Chinese printers using metal type. However, due to the complexity of the Chinese writing system, which contained thousands of unique characters, movable type printing did not achieve widespread adoption in East Asia.

Meanwhile, in the Islamic world, printing techniques were developing independently. The Middle Eastern printing industry flourished between the 12th and 14th centuries, with artisans using **block printing** to produce textiles, playing cards, and religious manuscripts. The Ottoman Empire, however, was slower to adopt movable type printing due to religious restrictions, which delayed the spread of printing in the region.

The most significant breakthrough in printing came in the 15th century with **Johannes Gutenberg's invention of the mechanical movable-type printing press** in Germany. His press, developed around 1440, used metal type pieces and an adjustable mold system, allowing for rapid and consistent reproduction of text. This innovation marked the beginning of mass production printing, as books could now be produced at an unprecedented rate. The first major book printed using this technology, the **Gutenberg Bible (1455),** demonstrated the potential of large-scale printing.

Gutenberg's printing press revolutionized communication, playing a crucial role in the **Renaissance, Reformation, and the Scientific Revolution.** Books, which were once hand-copied by scribes, became widely available, promoting literacy and the exchange of ideas across Europe. The press also enabled the rapid dissemination of Martin Luther's 95 Theses in 1517, which fueled the Protestant Reformation.

As printing technology continued to evolve, it became an essential tool for governments, businesses, and the scientific community. By the 17th century, newspapers began appearing in major European cities, providing the public with news, political commentary, and advertisements. The demand for printed materials increased significantly, leading to further innovations in press design and efficiency.

The **Industrial Revolution of the 19th century** brought mechanized printing presses, which enabled large-scale production and significantly reduced the cost of printed materials. The **steam-powered printing press**, introduced in 1814 by Friedrich Koenig, allowed newspapers such as *The Times* of London to print thousands of copies per hour, making print media more accessible than ever before. The development of the **rotary printing press** by Richard March Hoe in 1843 further improved speed and efficiency by using continuous rolls of paper instead of individual sheets.

By the late 19th and early 20th centuries, additional advancements such as the **linotype machine (1884)** revolutionized typesetting, allowing newspapers and books to be produced at a much faster rate. The introduction of **offset printing** in the early 20th century further improved print quality and cost efficiency, making it the dominant method for commercial printing.

In summary, the evolution of printing from ancient stamp seals to mechanized presses reflects humanity's continuous effort to improve communication, knowledge sharing, and mass production. The introduction of Gutenberg's press in the 15th century was a turning point, accelerating literacy and intellectual movements. The innovations of the 19th and 20th centuries transformed printing into a major industry, shaping modern education, journalism, and commerce.

As we enter the 21st century, printing technology continues to evolve, integrating digital and automated systems that further enhance efficiency and customization. Understanding the historical development of printing provides valuable insights into how this essential industry will continue to shape the future.

2.2 Key Milestones in the Printing Revolution

The history of printing is marked by numerous milestones that have shaped its evolution and expanded its role in communication, education, and commerce. Each advancement contributed to making printing more efficient, cost-effective, and widely accessible.

2.2.1 Gutenberg's Printing Press (1455)

Johannes Gutenberg's invention of the mechanical movable-type printing press in 1440 and the printing of the **Gutenberg Bible** in 1455 revolutionized the dissemination of knowledge. This innovation led to the rapid spread of literacy and academic inquiry across Europe, setting the foundation for mass communication.

2.2.2 Steam-Powered Printing Press (1814)

The introduction of the **steam-powered printing press** by Friedrich Koenig allowed newspapers, particularly *The Times* of London, to print over 1,000 pages per hour. This invention reduced the cost of printed materials and increased newspaper circulation, making news and literature more accessible to the public.

2.2.3 Rotary Printing Press (1843)

Richard March Hoe's invention of the **rotary printing press** in 1843 allowed for continuous printing from large paper rolls. This dramatically increased printing speed and was particularly influential in newspaper and magazine production.

2.2.4 Offset Printing (1860s)

Offset printing, developed in the late 19th century, improved image reproduction quality by transferring ink from a metal plate to a rubber blanket before applying it to paper. This method became the dominant printing technique for commercial use due to its high efficiency and cost-effectiveness.

2.2.5 Linotype Machine (1884)

The linotype machine, invented by Ottmar Mergenthaler, revolutionized typesetting by automating the arrangement of letters for printing. It significantly accelerated newspaper production and was widely used until the advent of digital publishing.

2.2.6 Phototypesetting and Computerized Printing (20th Century)

Advancements in phototypesetting and digital typography allowed for precise text and image reproduction. The development of laser printers and computer-controlled printing technologies enabled more detailed layouts and high-speed production.

2.2.7 Digital Printing (1990s)

The rise of digital printing technologies, such as inkjet and laser printing, enabled on-demand production and personalised content creation, reducing reliance on traditional printing plates. This advancement made printing more sustainable and efficient for short-run projects.

2.2.8 Milestones in Indian Printing History

The printing revolution in India followed a unique trajectory, influenced by colonial rule, regional linguistic diversity, and economic growth.

- **1556 – First Printing Press in India:** The Jesuit missionaries in Goa set up the first printing press in India to print Christian texts. The first book printed was *Doctrina Christam* in 1557.
- **1800 – Establishment of the Asiatic Society Press:** This press played a crucial role in publishing early Indian literature and historical texts.
- **1818 – First Bengali Newspaper:** The Bengal Gazette, also known as *Hicky's Bengal Gazette*, became India's first printed newspaper.
- **1864 – Lithographic Printing in India:** This method gained popularity for printing religious texts, especially in languages like Urdu, Persian, and Hindi.
- **1948 – Growth of Commercial Printing in Post-Independence India:** The publishing and newspaper industries expanded, supporting literacy and education.
- **1980s – Offset Printing Becomes Mainstream:** Offset printing gained dominance in India, revolutionizing the newspaper, packaging, and commercial printing sectors.
- **2000s – Digital Printing Boom:** With advancements in digital printing, small businesses and large-scale industries adopted digital presses for customized and short-run printing.

Each of these milestones played a critical role in shaping the Indian printing industry, making it one of the largest and most diverse print markets in the world today.

2.3 Major Technological Breakthroughs and Their Impact

The evolution of printing has been marked by technological breakthroughs that have transformed the industry:

- **Letterpress to Offset Printing:** Offset lithography, developed in the early 20th century, replaced letterpress printing as the dominant method due to its superior print quality and lower production costs.
- **Photographic and Laser Printing:** Photographic printing methods allowed for the reproduction of images with greater precision, leading to improved magazine and newspaper production. Laser printing, introduced in the 1970s, revolutionized office and commercial printing.
- **3D Printing:** The emergence of additive manufacturing, commonly known as 3D printing, has expanded the applications of printing beyond paper to include industrial design, healthcare, and engineering.
- **Artificial Intelligence (AI) and Automation:** AI-driven printing processes optimize efficiency by predicting maintenance needs, improving color management, and automating workflows.
- **Smart and Sustainable Printing:** Advances in eco-friendly materials, such as vegetable-based inks and recyclable paper, are making printing more sustainable. The integration of smart technologies, such as printed electronics and interactive packaging, is also redefining the role of print in the digital age.

These advancements continue to push the boundaries of what printing can achieve, ensuring its relevance in a rapidly evolving technological landscape.

2.4 The Transition from Conventional to Digital Printing

The printing industry has witnessed a remarkable transformation with the shift from traditional to digital printing methods. Conventional printing techniques, such as **offset, flexographic, gravure, and letterpress** printing, rely on mechanical processes that involve multiple steps, including plate-making, ink application, and extensive setup. These methods are highly efficient for large-scale production but often require significant time and resources, making them less suitable for short-run or customized printing.

Traditional Printing Methods and Their Limitations

1. **Offset Printing** – This technique involves transferring ink from a metal plate to a rubber blanket and then onto the printing surface. While offset printing is known for **exceptional image quality** and **cost-effectiveness in bulk production**, it requires **high setup costs**, making it impractical for small print runs.
2. **Flexographic Printing** – Commonly used for **packaging materials, labels, and flexible films,** flexographic printing uses flexible rubber plates. Although highly efficient for high-volume jobs, it lacks the flexibility for quick changes and variable data printing.
3. **Gravure Printing** – Often used for **magazines, wallpapers, and packaging,** gravure printing provides **consistent quality** but requires expensive engraved cylinders, making it ideal only for extremely high-volume production.
4. **Letterpress Printing** – One of the oldest methods, letterpress printing involves raised type surfaces for ink transfer. While it remains popular for **artistic and specialty printing,** it has largely been replaced by modern digital and offset methods due to its slow process and labor-intensive setup.

The Rise of Digital Printing

In contrast, **digital printing** eliminates the need for plates, making it possible to print directly from digital files onto various substrates. This innovation allows for:

- **Short-run printing** – Businesses and individuals can now print smaller quantities at affordable rates without the high costs associated with traditional printing.

- **On-demand printing** – Books, marketing materials, and packaging can be printed as needed, reducing storage costs and waste.
- **Variable data printing (VDP)** – Digital printing enables **customization and personalization**, allowing businesses to print unique copies with different text, images, or barcodes in a single print run.
- **Faster turnaround time** – Without the need for plate setup and drying time, digital printing provides **immediate output**, making it ideal for urgent projects.
- **Eco-friendliness** – Digital printing reduces **waste, energy consumption, and the use of chemicals**, making it a more sustainable option.

Impact on the Printing Industry

The shift from traditional to digital printing has transformed industries such as **publishing, packaging, advertising, and textiles**. While conventional printing still dominates **mass production**, digital printing is increasingly used for applications that require **customization, rapid delivery, and cost-effective short runs.**

By integrating **Artificial Intelligence (AI), automation, and advanced inkjet technologies**, digital printing continues to evolve, offering **enhanced efficiency, quality, and sustainability**. As businesses and consumers demand **faster, more flexible printing solutions**, digital printing will remain a driving force in the future of the industry.

Key Advantages of Digital Printing

The shift from conventional printing methods to **digital printing** has introduced numerous benefits, making printing faster, more cost-effective, and more sustainable. Below are some of the most significant advantages of digital printing:

1. On-Demand Production: Reducing Waste and Inventory Costs

One of the greatest advantages of digital printing is its ability to print **only what is needed, when it is needed.** Unlike traditional printing, which often requires bulk printing to be cost-effective, digital printing allows businesses and individuals to print in **small batches or even single copies** without incurring additional costs.

- **Reduces storage and inventory costs:** Since businesses don't have to print large quantities in advance, they can avoid stockpiling printed materials that may become outdated.
- **Minimizes waste:** Since materials are printed on demand, there is less risk of overproduction and obsolete inventory, making digital printing an efficient and cost-saving solution.
- **Ideal for books, marketing materials, and packaging:** On-demand printing is particularly beneficial for **self-publishing authors, product packaging, and limited-edition prints,** ensuring materials are always up to date.

2. Personalization and Variable Data Printing: Enhancing Customer Engagement

Unlike conventional printing methods that require uniform printing across all copies, **digital printing allows each printed piece to be unique.** This capability, known as **Variable Data Printing (VDP),** enables customization at an unprecedented scale.

- **Personalized marketing campaigns:** Businesses can tailor marketing materials such as brochures, postcards, and direct mailers with unique names, addresses, and promotional content specific to each recipient.

- Customized product packaging: Brands can create **limited edition packaging** with customer names, QR codes, or localized messaging, making products more appealing.
- Unique barcode and numbering applications: Digital printing is widely used for **lottery tickets, event tickets, and invoices**, where each printed piece needs to have a different serial number, barcode, or tracking code.

This level of personalization improves **customer engagement, response rates, and brand loyalty**, making digital printing an essential tool for modern marketing.

3. Faster Turnaround Times: Meeting Urgent Printing Needs

One of the biggest limitations of traditional printing is the **time-consuming setup** required for plates, ink mixing, and alignment. Digital printing eliminates these steps, significantly **reducing the time required to produce prints.**

- No pre-press setup: Since digital printing prints directly from a digital file, there is no need for **plate-making or lengthy** preparation.
- Immediate production: Unlike offset printing, which may take days to complete, digital printing can often produce **same-day or next-day prints.**
- Quick prototyping: Businesses can test **different designs** quickly without committing to large print runs, making digital printing ideal for **packaging prototypes, product labels, and advertising** materials.

This speed is crucial for businesses that need **quick marketing responses, last-minute promotional materials, or time-sensitive event invitations.**

4. Eco-Friendly Practices: A Sustainable Printing Solution

Sustainability has become a key consideration in modern printing, and digital printing offers a greener alternative compared to traditional printing methods.

- **Reduces chemical usage:** Unlike offset printing, which relies on chemical-based plates and solutions, digital printing eliminates the need for harmful chemicals, making the process cleaner and safer for the environment.
- **Lower energy consumption:** Digital printing consumes less energy since it does not require plate processing, ink drying, or complex machinery operation.
- **Less paper and ink waste:** With on-demand printing, there is less overproduction and fewer discarded prints, reducing the overall environmental impact.
- **Eco-friendly ink options:** Many digital printers now use water-based, UV-curable, and solvent-free inks, which are less toxic and biodegradable, making them a more sustainable option.

As businesses shift towards sustainable printing practices, digital printing continues to play a vital role in reducing carbon footprints, waste, and environmental impact.

Despite the advantages of digital printing, conventional methods still dominate certain sectors, such as high-volume newspaper printing, packaging, and specialty printing. Many companies now employ a hybrid approach, combining the strengths of both traditional and digital technologies to optimize production efficiency.

The transition to digital printing is not just a technological shift but also a response to changing consumer behavior. The demand for personalized content, eco-friendly solutions, and quick turnaround times has driven innovation in digital print technology, ensuring its continued growth in the future.

Digital printing is **revolutionizing the printing industry** by offering cost-effective, flexible, and sustainable solutions. Whether for **small businesses, large enterprises, or individual creators,** its on-demand capabilities, personalization options, fast production, and eco-friendly advantages make it a preferred choice in today's printing landscape. As **technology continues** to evolve, digital printing is expected to become even more **efficient, accessible, and innovative,** further transforming the way we produce printed materials.

Research Methodologies in Printing Studies

3.1 Overview of Research Approaches in Printing Technology

Research in printing technology plays a crucial role in advancing the industry by improving materials, optimizing processes, and integrating new technologies. Depending on the research objective, different methodologies are used to explore various aspects of printing, such as technical advancements, market trends, sustainability, and user behaviour.

The primary research approaches in printing technology include:

1. Experimental Research: Enhancing Print Quality and Efficiency

Definition:
Experimental research in printing technology involves controlled testing to examine the behaviour of different variables, such as printing inks, substrates, print quality, and machinery performance. This approach is commonly used in laboratories and industrial settings to assess how different printing techniques influence durability, color accuracy, and efficiency.

Applications in Printing Technology:

- **Ink and Substrate Compatibility Testing:** Researchers test different inks (e.g., UV-curable, water-based, solvent-based) on various **substrates** (e.g., paper, plastic, metal, textiles) to ensure quality and durability.
- **Optimization of Print Parameters:** Studies analyze factors such as **ink viscosity, drying time, curing processes, and resolution** to improve **print clarity and consistency.**
- **New Printing Technologies:** Experimental research is used to develop and refine **3D printing, nanographic printing, and high-speed inkjet systems** for industrial applications.
- **Sustainability Studies:** This approach is also used to test eco-**friendly inks and recycled paper,** contributing to the shift towards **green printing practices.**

Example:
A study testing the **adhesion of biodegradable ink on recycled paper** under different drying conditions helps manufacturers develop **more sustainable** printing solutions.

2. **Analytical Research: Identifying Industry Trends and Market Patterns**

Definition:
Analytical research focuses on **data collection, statistical modeling, and trend analysis** to understand patterns in **technology adoption, consumer preferences, and industry performance.** This type of research helps businesses and researchers make informed decisions about **printing investments and innovations.**

Applications in Printing Technology:

- Market Trends and Adoption Rates: Identifies how quickly digital printing technologies (e.g., inkjet, laser, and UV printing) are replacing traditional methods.
- Cost-Benefit Analysis: Compares production costs, efficiency, and profit margins of digital vs. offset printing.
- Consumer Preferences: Surveys and data analysis help understand customer behavior, such as preferences for personalized printing, eco-friendly packaging, and high-quality print products.
- Competitive Analysis: Research helps businesses evaluate competitor pricing, service offerings, and technological capabilities in the printing industry.

Example:
A comparative analysis of offset printing vs. digital printing in commercial book publishing may reveal that digital printing is gaining popularity due to its ability to handle short print runs and personalized content efficiently.

3. Applied Research: Solving Industry Challenges with Practical Solutions

Definition:
Applied research directly addresses industry-specific challenges and innovations, bridging the gap between theoretical knowledge and practical application. This approach focuses on problem-solving and process improvements in commercial and industrial printing.

Applications in Printing Technology:

- Development of New Printing Methods: Innovations like hybrid printing (combining offset and digital printing) help industries improve cost efficiency and flexibility.

- Automation in Printing: Research on **robotic automation, AI-driven quality control, and workflow optimization** enhances productivity in large-scale printing operations.
- Sustainable Printing Innovations: Applied research focuses on **reducing ink waste, developing bio-based inks, and improving energy-efficient printing techniques.**
- Customized Printing Solutions: Research helps industries **personalize printing** for **marketing campaigns, packaging, and security printing (e.g., anti-counterfeit labels, RFID tags, and holograms).**

Example:

An applied research project on **UV-curable inks** led to the development of faster-drying, solvent-free inks that are now widely used in **label printing and commercial packaging.**

4. Combining Research Approaches for Comprehensive Insights

While **experimental, analytical, and applied research** each have distinct purposes, they are often **combined** to provide **holistic solutions** to industry challenges.

Example of an Integrated Research Study:

Research Topic: Improving the Efficiency of Eco-Friendly Inkjet Printing

1. **Experimental Research:** Tests various biodegradable inks on different substrates to measure **color accuracy, adhesion, and durability.**
2. **Analytical Research:** Evaluates **market demand** and **cost-effectiveness** of eco-friendly inks compared to traditional inks.
3. **Applied Research:** Develops a **practical solution** by optimizing ink **formulation and printer settings** for commercial adoption.

By merging these approaches, researchers can develop practical innovations, improve industry efficiency, and contribute to sustainable printing solutions.

The printing industry benefits greatly from a combination of research methodologies. While experimental research enhances technology and processes, analytical research helps identify trends and market opportunities. Applied research then turns these insights into real-world solutions that improve printing quality, efficiency, and sustainability.

By adopting these approaches, researchers and industry professionals can continue to drive innovation and maintain the relevance of printing technology in the digital age.

3.2 Quantitative and Qualitative Research Methods

Research in printing studies requires both quantitative and qualitative methods to provide a comprehensive understanding of technological advancements, market trends, consumer behavior, and operational efficiency. While quantitative methods rely on numerical data and statistical analysis, qualitative methods focus on subjective insights gained from observations, interviews, and case studies.

A mixed-method approach, which combines both quantitative and qualitative research, is often the most effective strategy for exploring complex issues in the printing industry. By integrating objective measurements with real-world insights, researchers can develop a more holistic understanding of challenges and opportunities in printing technology.

1. Quantitative Research Methods: Measuring Printing Efficiency and Market Trends

Definition:

Quantitative research in printing studies involves **numerical data, structured surveys, statistical modeling, and controlled experiments** to measure **performance, efficiency, and trends.** This method is valuable for testing hypotheses and making data-driven conclusions about **printing processes, materials, and market demands.**

Applications of Quantitative Research in Printing Technology

i. Printing Efficiency and Performance Analysis

- Researchers conduct **controlled experiments** to measure **print resolution, drying time, ink adhesion, and durability** under different conditions.
- **Example:** Testing how **UV-curable inks** perform under varying temperatures and humidity levels.

ii. Market and Consumer Behavior Surveys

- **Large-scale surveys** collect data from **print buyers, industry professionals, and consumers** to analyze preferences for **digital vs. offset printing, eco-friendly materials, and personalized packaging.**
- **Example:** A study that surveys **1,000 print businesses** to determine the **adoption rate of digital printing technologies.**

iii. Cost-Benefit and Return on Investment (ROI) Analysis

- Researchers use **economic modeling and cost analysis** to compare the **expenses of traditional vs. digital printing** and determine the **long-term profitability of automation in print shops.**
- **Example:** A financial study comparing **flexographic vs. digital printing** in the packaging industry.

iv. Big Data and Statistical Modeling in Printing

- Statistical software (SPSS, R, Python) is used to analyze market trends, customer preferences, and production efficiency.
- Example: Predicting future demand for sustainable printing solutions based on historical sales data.

2. Qualitative Research Methods: Exploring Industry Insights and Technological Challenges

Definition:

Qualitative research in printing technology focuses on subjective insights, expert opinions, case studies, and observational research to explore industry challenges, user experiences, and emerging trends.

Applications of Qualitative Research in Printing Technology

i. Expert Interviews and Industry Insight

- Direct interviews with printing professionals, manufacturers, and researchers provide in-depth insights into technological adoption, challenges in automation, and market needs.
- Example: An interview with a print shop owner discussing the challenges of integrating AI-driven workflow automation.

ii. Case Studies of Technological Advancements

- Case studies focus on real-world applications of printing innovations, such as successful implementations of variable data printing or sustainable inks.
- Example: A case study on a leading newspaper company that successfully transitioned from offset to digital printing for cost efficiency and flexibility.

iii. Observational Research in Print Production

- Researchers visit **printing facilities, packaging plants, and press rooms** to observe **workflow efficiency, waste management, and operator challenges.**
- **Example:** Observing how **3D printing is being used in prototype development** for packaging designs.

iv. User-Centric Research on Printed Materials

- Focus groups and interviews assess **consumer engagement with printed advertisements, books, and packaging** to understand the psychological impact of print designs and color choices.
- **Example:** A study exploring **how different packaging designs influence consumer purchasing decisions** in retail stores.

3. Mixed-Method Approach: Combining Quantitative and Qualitative Research

While **quantitative research** provides objective data and measurable trends, qualitative research helps **interpret and explain** these findings with real-world insights. Many printing studies use a **mixed-method approach** to gain **both statistical accuracy and industry perspectives.**
Example of a Mixed-Method Study

Research Topic: Adoption of AI-Driven Printing Technologies in Commercial Print Shops

1. Quantitative Analysis:

- Conducting a **survey with 500 printing companies** to measure the **percentage of businesses using AI-driven workflow automation.**
- Using **statistical analysis** to predict future **adoption trends.**

2. Qualitative Analysis:

- Conducting interviews with print shop owners to understand the challenges and benefits of AI integration.
- Observing workflow improvements in a printing facility before and after AI implementation.

3. Final Insights:

- The combined research reveals that while AI improves efficiency, smaller print businesses struggle with cost barriers and training issues.

Both quantitative and qualitative research methods play essential roles in printing studies. Quantitative methods provide data-driven insights, while qualitative methods explore the context and experiences behind those numbers. By using a mixed-method approach, researchers can gain a comprehensive perspective on the technological, economic, and user-centric aspects of the printing industry.

3.3 Case Studies and Industry Surveys

Research in printing technology benefits significantly from case studies and industry surveys, which provide real-world insights into technological advancements, market trends, and business strategies. These methods help researchers understand industry challenges, evaluate the effectiveness of innovations, and identify future growth opportunities.

1. Case Studies: In-Depth Analysis of Printing Technologies and Business Models

Definition:

A case study is an in-depth exploration of a specific company, technology, process, or project in the printing industry. It provides detailed qualitative and quantitative insights into the challenges, successes, and outcomes of adopting new printing solutions.

Applications of Case Studies in Printing Technology

1. Transition from Offset to Digital Printing

- A case study can explore how a publishing house shifted from traditional offset printing to digital printing to meet the growing demand for on-demand and personalized books.
- **Key Insights:**
- Cost-effectiveness of digital printing for small print runs.
- Reduction in waste and inventory costs.
- Improved customer satisfaction through customization.

2. Implementation of AI in Print Production

- A detailed study of a commercial print shop integrating AI-based workflow automation to optimize job scheduling, color calibration, and print quality control.
- **Key Insights:**
- Increased operational efficiency.
- Reduction in human errors and setup times.
- Challenges related to training employees on AI-driven systems.

3. Sustainable Printing Practices in Packaging

- A case study of a packaging company adopting eco-friendly inks, biodegradable materials, and energy-efficient presses to reduce carbon footprint.
- Key Insights:
- Consumer preference for sustainable packaging.
- Regulatory compliance and certifications required.
- Long-term cost savings vs. initial investment challenges.

4. Growth of 3D Printing in Prototyping and Manufacturing

- Analyzing how a printing company uses 3D printing for rapid prototyping in industries like automotive, medical packaging, and fashion.
- Key Insights:
- Time and cost benefits in prototyping.
- Expansion of 3D printing applications beyond prototyping into end-use production.

5. Impact of Variable Data Printing (VDP) on Marketing Campaigns

- A case study on a direct mail marketing company that implemented variable data printing (VDP) to personalize advertisements for targeted customer engagement.
- Key Insights:
- Increased response rates and ROI from personalized campaigns.
- Technical challenges in integrating data management systems with digital presses.

2. Industry Surveys: Large-Scale Data Collection on Printing Trends

Definition:
Industry surveys involve gathering structured data from professionals, companies, and organizations in the printing sector to analyze current

trends, challenges, and future projections. These surveys help policymakers, researchers, and business leaders make informed decisions based on industry-wide insights.

Applications of Industry Surveys in Printing Technology

1. Adoption of Digital Printing Technologies

- A survey of 500 commercial print shops analyzing the adoption rate of digital printing solutions, including inkjet and laser-based technologies.
- **Key Findings:**
- Growth in digital printing adoption across publishing, packaging, and textiles.
- Barriers such as high initial investment costs and the need for skilled labor.

2. Sustainability Trends in Printing

- A global industry survey examining the impact of eco-friendly initiatives, such as water-based inks, recycled paper, and carbon-neutral printing processes.
- **Key Findings:**
- Increasing consumer demand for green printing solutions.
- Challenges related to cost and material availability.

3. Integration of Artificial Intelligence (AI) in Print Production

- A survey of printing professionals assessing the role of AI in automation, predictive maintenance, and workflow optimization.
- **Key Findings:**
- AI is mainly used for prepress automation and color management.
- Smaller print businesses face barriers in AI adoption due to high costs and lack of expertise.

4. Growth of 3D Printing in Industrial Applications

- An industry-wide survey on 3D printing applications in automotive, healthcare, and packaging.
- Key Findings:
- Increased investment in 3D printing for mass production.
- Challenges related to material costs and regulatory approvals.

5. Impact of Personalization on Print Marketing

- A survey of advertising agencies and print service providers measuring the effectiveness of personalized print campaigns.
- Key Findings:
- Higher engagement and conversion rates in personalized direct mail campaigns.
- Advances in variable data printing (VDP) and AI-driven customization.

3. Combining Case Studies and Surveys for Comprehensive Insights

Both case studies and industry surveys provide valuable insights into technological advancements, market dynamics, and industry challenges. While case studies offer in-depth analysis of specific implementations, surveys provide large-scale statistical validation of trends.

Example of a Combined Study
Research Topic: The Future of Sustainable Printing in Commercial Print Shops
1. Case Study Component:

- Analyzing how a leading print company successfully transitioned to sustainable ink and paper while maintaining profitability.

2. Survey Component:

- Conducting a global survey of 1,000 printing businesses to assess the adoption rate of eco-friendly printing technologies.

3. Final Insights:

- While case studies reveal success strategies for sustainability, surveys confirm that cost barriers remain a major challenge for industry-wide adoption.

Both case studies and industry surveys are essential for understanding the evolution of printing technologies. Case studies offer detailed, real-world insights into specific printing innovations, while industry surveys provide large-scale statistical validation of trends. By integrating both methods, researchers can generate comprehensive insights that drive technological advancements, business strategies, and policy decisions in the printing industry.

3.4 Data Collection Techniques and Analysis

Effective research in **printing technology** relies on a combination of **quantitative and qualitative data collection techniques** to ensure accuracy and reliability. These methods help researchers evaluate **technological advancements, market trends, and industry challenges**. The data collected is then analyzed using **statistical tools, qualitative assessment techniques, and data visualization methods** to derive **meaningful insights**.

1. Data Collection Techniques

1.1 Experimental Data Collection

Experimental research involves **testing and measuring physical properties, performance, and efficiency** under controlled conditions. This method is essential for improving **printing materials, ink formulations, and press operations.**

Applications in Printing Research:

- Ink Performance Testing:
- Measuring **viscosity, adhesion, and drying time** of different ink formulations.
- Analyzing the **impact of temperature and humidity on print** quality.

- Print Durability Assessment:
- Conducting **abrasion and rub resistance tests** to measure print longevity.
- Evaluating the **fade resistance of UV-curable and eco-solvent inks** under prolonged exposure to light.

- Energy Efficiency Testing:
- Measuring the **power consumption of digital vs. offset printing** machines.
- Assessing the impact of **AI-driven automation on reducing energy** waste.

1.2 Surveys and Questionnaires

Surveys and questionnaires are commonly used to gather **opinions, preferences, and experiences** from **print business owners, consumers, suppliers, and industry experts.** These tools help understand **market trends, customer satisfaction,** and technology adoption rates.

Key Areas of Survey Research:

- Digital Printing Adoption:
- Surveying print businesses about the challenges and benefits of switching from traditional to digital printing.

- Sustainability in Printing:
- Gathering data on the use of recycled materials, eco-friendly inks, and energy-efficient equipment.

- AI and Automation in Print Workflows:
- Measuring industry readiness for AI-driven job scheduling, predictive maintenance, and automated prepress workflows.

1.3 Market Analysis

Market analysis involves examining financial data, trade reports, and industry publications to identify trends, growth opportunities, and economic challenges in the printing sector.

Sources of Market Data:

- Industry Reports:
- Data from printing associations, market research firms, and government reports.

- Financial Data:
- Revenue trends of leading printing companies to track the growth of digital printing.

- Trade Publications and Conferences:
- Articles from print technology magazines and insights from printing expos and summits.

1.4 Focus Groups and Interviews

Focus groups and interviews provide **in-depth qualitative insights** by engaging directly with **industry professionals, researchers, and end-users.** These methods help explore **emerging trends, potential risks, and** innovation opportunities.

Key Focus Areas for Interviews:

- AI-Driven Printing Automation:
- Experts discuss how **machine learning is transforming** color **management and print scheduling.**

- Sustainable Printing Innovations:
- Suppliers share insights on **biodegradable packaging materials and water-based inks.**

- Future of 3D Printing in Commercial Applications:
- Exploring how **3D printing is impacting prototyping, product packaging, and customization.**

2. Data Analysis Techniques

Once data is collected, it must be processed and analyzed using **statistical and qualitative techniques** to derive useful conclusions.

2.1 Statistical Analysis

Statistical tools help **interpret numerical data and identify trends**. Common techniques include:

- Descriptive Statistics:
- Summarizing survey responses, such as **percentage of print shops using digital printing**.

- Regression Analysis:
- Identifying **factors influencing print quality**, such as ink viscosity vs. drying time.

- Time Series Analysis:
- Examining **historical data on print technology adoption rates** over the years.

2.2 Qualitative Analysis

Qualitative methods are used to **analyze textual data** from interviews, focus groups, and case studies. Common techniques include:

- Thematic Analysis:
- Identifying recurring themes in expert discussions, such as **barriers to AI adoption in printing**.

- Content Analysis:
- Examining industry reports and trade magazines for **mentions of sustainability practices**.

2.3 Data Visualization

To enhance data presentation and decision-making, results are often visualized using:

- Graphs and Charts:
- Line graphs to show trends in digital printing adoption.
- Pie charts to illustrate the market share of different printing technologies.

- Heatmaps and Infographics:
- Highlighting geographical variations in print industry growth.

Reliable data collection and analysis are crucial for advancing printing technology research. By integrating experimental data, surveys, market analysis, and qualitative interviews, researchers can gain comprehensive insights into industry trends, challenges, and future opportunities. Using statistical and visualization tools ensures that the findings are accurate, actionable, and relevant for both academia and industry professionals.

Trends in Technological Growth

4.1 Introduction

The printing industry has undergone a profound transformation over the past few decades, driven by rapid technological advancements, digitalization, automation, and shifting market demands. The transition from traditional printing methods to digital and AI-driven processes has revolutionized production efficiency, cost-effectiveness, and environmental sustainability. Understanding these changes requires a comprehensive analysis of data trends, technological innovations, and industry growth patterns.

Data analysis plays a crucial role in identifying emerging technologies, evaluating their impact, and predicting future advancements in the printing industry. With the increasing integration of artificial intelligence, automation, and sustainable practices, businesses and researchers rely on data-driven insights to navigate the evolving landscape of printing technology. This chapter explores the various sources of data, research methodologies, and key trends influencing technological growth in the printing sector. It focuses on areas such as digital printing, 3D printing, AI-based automation, and green printing initiatives, providing a holistic view of the industry's trajectory.

4.2 Analytical Methods

To assess technological growth in the printing industry, researchers and industry analysts rely on various data collection and analysis techniques. These include:

4.2.1 Data Collection Methods

- **Industry Reports & Market Studies:** Reports from organizations such as FICCI, AIFMP, and global market research firms provide insights into technology adoption, investment trends, and economic impact. These reports often contain statistical data, growth projections, and comparative studies of printing technologies.
- **Surveys and Questionnaires:** Data from printing businesses, suppliers, and consumers help assess industry needs and innovation adoption. These tools enable researchers to capture real-time feedback on the effectiveness and challenges of emerging printing technologies.
- **Experimental Research:** Lab tests on ink formulations, print durability, and energy efficiency provide empirical data for evaluating new technologies. Controlled experiments help refine printing methods and enhance the quality and longevity of printed materials.
- **Market Analysis:** Reviewing financial reports, trade publications, and production statistics aids in understanding economic and competitive shifts. This method helps identify patterns in industry revenue, investment in new technologies, and market demand fluctuations.
- **Expert Interviews and Focus Groups:** Engaging with printing technocrats, industry professionals, and academic researchers provides qualitative insights into challenges and future prospects.

Focus groups facilitate in-depth discussions on industry trends, regulatory impacts, and anticipated technological advancements.

4.2.2 Analytical Approaches

- **Statistical Forecasting Models:** Time series analysis, regression models, and predictive analytics are used to assess historical data trends and predict future technological growth in printing. These models help businesses anticipate market shifts and make data-driven investment decisions.
- **Market Segmentation Analysis:** This method categorizes the printing industry into different segments such as packaging, publishing, textile printing, and 3D printing. It helps identify sector-specific growth patterns, demand drivers, and technological adoption rates.
- **Comparative Technology Assessment:** Evaluates different printing methods (offset, flexographic, gravure, and digital) based on key factors such as cost-effectiveness, efficiency, quality, and environmental impact. This analysis aids businesses in selecting the most suitable printing solutions for their needs.
- **SWOT Analysis:** A strategic tool used to examine the strengths, weaknesses, opportunities, and threats associated with emerging printing technologies. It helps companies identify competitive advantages and mitigate potential risks in technology adoption.

4.3.1 The Shift from Conventional to Digital Printing

The transition from traditional printing (offset, flexographic, and gravure) to digital printing is one of the most significant trends shaping the industry. Digital printing has gained popularity due to its ability to handle short-run jobs, enable variable data printing, and reduce waste.

Key Drivers of Digital Printing Growth:

- **On-Demand Printing:** Traditional printing methods require large print runs to be cost-effective. Digital printing, however, allows businesses to produce prints only as needed, reducing inventory costs and waste. This shift is particularly beneficial for industries like publishing, where short-run and self-publishing models are gaining traction.
- **Variable Data Printing (VDP):** Unlike conventional printing, digital printing enables each printed piece to be unique. This capability is widely used in direct mail campaigns, personalized marketing materials, and custom packaging, allowing brands to target customers more effectively.
- **Advancements in Inkjet and Toner Technologies:** Innovations in inkjet and electrophotographic printing have significantly improved speed, resolution, and cost-effectiveness. High-speed inkjet printers now compete with traditional offset presses in terms of quality and throughput, making digital printing viable for larger-scale commercial applications.
- **Eco-Friendly Benefits:** Digital printing eliminates the need for printing plates and chemical processing, reducing environmental impact. Water-based and UV-curable inks further contribute to sustainability by minimizing emissions and hazardous waste. Additionally, digital processes consume less energy than traditional printing methods, aligning with the industry's push toward greener production techniques.

Key Drivers of Digital Printing Growth:

- **On-Demand Printing:** Businesses prioritize personalized, short-run prints over bulk offset jobs.
- **Variable Data Printing (VDP):** Enables targeted marketing and customization in publishing and packaging.

- **Advancements in Inkjet and Toner Technologies:** Enhances speed, quality, and cost-effectiveness, making digital printing competitive with offset.
- **Eco-Friendly Benefits:** Digital printing minimizes chemical use, energy consumption, and material waste.

4.3.2 The Rise of 3D Printing and Printed Electronics

The evolution of printing technology has extended beyond traditional 2D applications, paving the way for 3D printing and printed electronics. These advancements are transforming industries by enabling rapid prototyping, personalized manufacturing, and the integration of electronic functionalities into printed products. Innovations in material science, automation, and digital workflows have accelerated the adoption of these technologies, opening new opportunities for commercial and industrial applications.

3D Printing in the Printing Industry

3D printing, also known as additive manufacturing, involves building three-dimensional objects layer by layer from digital designs. Unlike conventional subtractive manufacturing methods, which cut or shape raw materials into desired forms, 3D printing minimizes material waste and allows for highly customizable production.

Key Benefits of 3D Printing in the Printing Industry

- **Rapid Prototyping** – Shortens product development cycles by allowing designers to create, test, and refine prototypes quickly.
- **Customization & Personalization** – Enables the creation of unique, one-of-a-kind products without costly setup changes.
- **Reduced Waste & Sustainability** – Additive manufacturing uses

only the necessary amount of material, reducing excess waste compared to traditional manufacturing.

- **Cost-Effective Short Runs** – Ideal for small-batch production, avoiding the high setup costs of traditional mass manufacturing.

Applications of 3D Printing in Printing Technology

1. Packaging Industry

The packaging sector is leveraging 3D printing for rapid prototyping, structural design testing, and personalized packaging solutions.

- **Prototype Development:** Packaging companies can create physical models of labels, cartons, and containers before committing to large-scale production.
- **Customization:** Brands are experimenting with 3D-printed embossed packaging, allowing for intricate textures and raised lettering to enhance the user experience.
- **Sustainable Packaging:** Researchers are exploring 3D-printed biodegradable materials to reduce plastic waste in packaging.

2. Medical & Healthcare Industry

The medical sector has seen groundbreaking applications of 3D printing, revolutionizing patient care and biomedical research.

- **3D-Printed Prosthetics:** Custom prosthetics can be manufactured with precision to fit individual patients, improving comfort and functionality.
- **Bio-Printing for Organ Research:** Scientists are working on printing tissues, blood vessels, and even organ structures,

advancing regenerative medicine.

- **Surgical Models & Guides:** Physicians use 3D-printed anatomical models for surgical planning and training, improving accuracy and patient outcomes.

3. Manufacturing Industry

3D printing is reshaping industrial manufacturing by enabling the production of tools, components, and customized products.

- **Custom Tooling & Spare Parts:** Industries use 3D printing to create specialized tools and replacement parts on demand, reducing downtime and inventory costs.
- **Automotive & Aerospace Applications:** Car manufacturers and aerospace companies use 3D printing to fabricate lightweight, durable components for enhanced fuel efficiency.
- **Industrial Prototyping:** Companies develop functional prototypes of mechanical parts to test designs before committing to mass production.

Printed Electronics in the Printing Industry

Printed electronics involve the use of conductive inks and flexible substrates to produce electronic circuits and components through printing processes. This technology enables the mass production of lightweight, flexible, and cost-effective electronic devices that integrate seamlessly into various applications.

Key Benefits of Printed Electronics

- **Low-Cost Production:** Printed electronics reduce manufacturing costs by using roll-to-roll printing techniques, eliminating complex assembly steps.

- **Flexible & Lightweight:** Unlike traditional rigid electronic components, printed electronics can be integrated into flexible materials, expanding design possibilities.
- **Scalability:** High-speed printing methods allow for mass production of electronic circuits, making the technology suitable for consumer electronics, packaging, and healthcare applications.

Applications of Printed Electronics in Printing Technology

1. Flexible Displays & Wearable Electronics

- **E-Paper & Smart Displays:** Printed electronics enable the development of flexible, paper-thin e-readers and smart labels that display real-time information.
- **Wearable Sensors:** Printed circuits are used in health monitoring devices, such as smart clothing and fitness trackers, providing real-time biometric data.

2. RFID Tags & Smart Packaging

- **Radio-Frequency Identification (RFID) Tags:** These are embedded into product packaging to track inventory, prevent counterfeiting, and enhance supply chain management.
- **Smart Labels:** Interactive printed electronics allow labels to change dynamically based on temperature, freshness, or external stimuli.
- **QR Code & NFC Integration:** Some packaging solutions now include printed NFC (Near Field Communication) technology, allowing consumers to access digital content by scanning labels with their smartphones.

3. Conductive Ink & Circuit Printing

- **Printed Batteries & Sensors:** Conductive inks enable the printing of lightweight, ultra-thin batteries and environmental sensors for industrial applications.

- **Flexible Circuit Boards:** Printed circuit boards (PCBs) using conductive inks are used in next-generation consumer electronics, reducing weight and material costs.

Future Outlook for 3D Printing & Printed Electronics

The advancements in 3D printing and printed electronics are expected to drive further innovation in the printing industry. The following trends will shape the future:

- **Increased Adoption in Packaging:** The use of 3D-printed molds, embossing, and smart packaging will continue to grow, enhancing product security and consumer engagement.
- **Advancements in Bioprinting:** The development of 3D-printed tissues and organs will push the boundaries of medical research and healthcare solutions.
- **Integration with IoT:** Printed electronics will play a crucial role in smart devices and the Internet of Things (IoT), allowing for seamless connectivity in everyday products.
- **Sustainability & Material Innovations:** The industry will focus on biodegradable, eco-friendly materials to align with global sustainability efforts.

The rise of 3D printing and printed electronics marks a significant shift in the printing industry, merging traditional printing techniques with cutting-edge manufacturing and electronic applications. These technologies are enhancing efficiency, enabling customization, and expanding the functionality of printed materials beyond conventional limits. As advancements continue, their impact will be felt across multiple sectors, reinforcing the printing industry's role in the digital and technological revolution.

4.3.3 Automation and AI in Print Production

The printing industry is undergoing a significant transformation with the integration of Artificial Intelligence (AI) and automation in production workflows. These technologies are streamlining operations, reducing costs, and enhancing overall efficiency. Traditional printing processes often involve manual intervention, which can lead to inefficiencies, errors, and high labor costs. AI and automation address these challenges by introducing smart workflows, predictive analytics, and robotic systems, enabling faster, more precise, and cost-effective printing solutions.

The adoption of AI and automation is especially crucial in an era where on-demand printing, digital workflows, and mass customization are becoming standard industry requirements. These innovations are being implemented across various stages of print production, including prepress, press, and post-press processes.

Key AI-Driven Innovations in Print Production

1. Automated Prepress Workflows
Prepress is one of the most critical stages in printing, involving design layout, color management, file preparation, and plate creation. AI-driven software is revolutionizing this process by automating repetitive tasks and reducing the need for manual intervention.

- Automated Color Correction: AI-based software analyzes images and automatically adjusts color levels, contrast, and sharpness to ensure consistent print quality.
- Layout Optimization: Intelligent algorithms optimize page layouts to minimize paper waste and reduce printing costs.
- Error Detection: AI tools detect potential issues such as low-resolution images, misalignment, and font compatibility problems

before printing, reducing reprints and material waste.
- Preflight Checking: AI automates preflight inspections to ensure that files meet printing specifications, preventing costly production errors.

Example: Many commercial printing companies use AI-powered workflow automation tools like EFI Fiery, Heidelberg Prinect, and Agfa Apogee to streamline prepress operations and enhance print accuracy.

2. Predictive Maintenance for Printing Equipment

Printing presses and machinery require regular maintenance to ensure smooth operation. Unexpected breakdowns can cause production delays, financial losses, and operational inefficiencies. AI-powered predictive maintenance systems help prevent equipment failures by continuously monitoring performance and detecting issues before they escalate.

- Smart Sensors & IoT Integration: AI-driven sensors collect real-time data on temperature, vibration, pressure, and ink levels, identifying early signs of wear and tear.
- Failure Prediction & Preventive Repairs: Machine learning models analyze past performance data to predict when parts will need maintenance, allowing proactive repairs and reducing downtime.
- Automated Service Scheduling: AI systems can schedule maintenance tasks without disrupting production, optimizing service intervals to extend the lifespan of printing machinery.

Example: Leading press manufacturers such as Heidelberg, Komori, and HP Indigo incorporate AI-driven predictive maintenance solutions to minimize operational disruptions and improve efficiency.

3. AI-Enhanced Color Management

Color consistency is essential in printing, especially for packaging, branding, and commercial printing. Variations in color output across different devices and substrates can lead to costly reprints and customer dissatisfaction. AI-driven color management solutions are addressing these challenges by ensuring accurate color reproduction.

- Intelligent Color Matching: AI algorithms analyze images and automatically adjust CMYK, RGB, or spot colors to maintain consistency across print jobs.
- Adaptive Color Correction: AI systems adapt to different paper types, inks, and printing conditions, optimizing color fidelity in real-time.
- Automated Proofing & Quality Control: AI tools compare digital proofs with final prints to detect color deviations and ensure brand consistency.

Example: Pantone and X-Rite i1Pro use AI to ensure precision in color matching, allowing brands to maintain their signature colors across various printing methods.

4. Robotic Printing Solutions

The introduction of robotics in print production is enhancing efficiency, reducing human intervention, and improving workflow automation. Robotic arms, autonomous printing stations, and AI-driven print operators are transforming various aspects of the printing process.

- Automated Printing Press Operations: Robots handle repetitive tasks such as paper loading, plate changing, and ink refilling, reducing labor costs and increasing production speed.

- 3D Printing Automation: AI-driven robotic arms facilitate multi-material 3D printing, improving precision and consistency in additive manufacturing applications.
- Post-Press & Finishing Automation: Robots assist with cutting, binding, folding, and packaging, ensuring high-speed and accurate finishing operations.

Example: Canon, Ricoh, and Xerox have developed robotic printing systems that integrate AI-powered automation to improve production efficiency and reduce human intervention.

Benefits of AI and Automation in Print Production

1. Increased Efficiency & Speed

AI and automation streamline printing workflows, reducing turnaround times and increasing production capacity. Tasks that once took hours can now be completed in minutes, enabling faster job processing and delivery.

2. Cost Reduction

By minimizing manual labor, reducing waste, and optimizing resource usage, AI-driven automation lowers operational costs and improves profitability.

3. Improved Print Quality

AI-enhanced color management, automated quality control, and intelligent layout adjustments ensure consistent and high-quality print output across different jobs and substrates.

4. Enhanced Sustainability

Automation reduces paper waste, optimizes ink usage, and improves energy efficiency, aligning with green printing initiatives and eco-friendly practices.

5. Seamless Mass Customization

AI-driven workflows enable personalized and variable data printing, allowing brands to customize marketing materials, packaging, and labels at scale.

Future Trends in AI and Automation for Printing

Looking ahead, AI and automation will continue to reshape the printing industry in the following ways:

AI-Powered Smart Printing Factories – Fully automated print shops with minimal human intervention, optimizing job scheduling and print production in real-time.

Integration with IoT & Cloud Computing – AI will connect print production systems to the cloud, enabling remote monitoring, automated job tracking, and seamless data exchange.

AI-Driven Quality Assurance – Advanced computer vision and machine learning will detect defects in prints and automatically adjust settings for perfect output.

Autonomous Robotic Printing Presses – The development of self-operating presses that adjust ink levels, replace components, and optimize print quality autonomously.

The incorporation of AI and automation in print production is redefining the industry, making processes more efficient, cost-effective, and environmentally sustainable. From automated prepress workflows to predictive maintenance and robotic solutions, these technologies are optimizing every stage of the printing process. As AI continues to evolve, it will unlock even greater potential for smart, connected, and highly efficient print production environments. Businesses that embrace these innovations will stay ahead in the competitive printing landscape, ensuring higher productivity, superior quality, and increased profitability.

4.3.4 Sustainability and Green Printing Initiatives

With growing environmental concerns and increasing regulatory pressures, the printing industry is making a **significant shift towards sustainability.** Traditional printing processes often involve **high energy consumption, chemical waste, and non-recyclable materials,** which contribute to pollution and resource depletion. However, the industry is actively adopting eco-friendly practices, sustainable materials, and energy-efficient technologies to reduce its environmental impact.

Sustainability in printing is no longer just an option—it has become a **business necessity** as companies strive to meet environmental regulations, reduce operational costs, and align with consumer demand for eco-conscious products. Green printing initiatives focus on **reducing waste, lowering emissions, and utilizing renewable resources,** ensuring a more sustainable future for the industry.

Key Sustainability Trends in Printing

1. Eco-Friendly Inks

Traditional petroleum-based inks contain **volatile organic compounds (VOCs), heavy metals, and toxic solvents,** which can contribute to air pollution, soil contamination, and health hazards for workers. In response, the industry has shifted towards environmentally friendly ink alternatives, including:

Water-Based Inks

- Contain **no harmful solvents** and emit significantly fewer VOCs.
- Widely used in **flexographic and inkjet printing** for packaging, textiles, and paper-based products.
- Offer **fast drying** and **high-quality color vibrancy** without compromising performance.

Soy-Based Inks

- Made from **renewable soy oil**, replacing petroleum-based alternatives.
- Produce **brighter and sharper colors** due to better pigment dispersion.
- More **biodegradable and easier to de-ink**, making paper recycling more efficient.
- Commonly used in **newspaper, magazine, and commercial printing**.

UV-Curable Inks

- Dry instantly when exposed to **ultraviolet (UV) light**, eliminating the need for solvent evaporation.
- **No VOC emissions**, reducing air pollution.
- Used in **digital, offset, and flexographic printing** for labels, packaging, and signage.
- UV inks are known for their **durability, scratch resistance, and vibrant colors**.

Example: Major printing companies like **Heidelberg, HP, and Fujifilm** have developed water-based and UV-curable ink solutions to support sustainability in commercial printing.

2. Recyclable & Biodegradable Substrates

The choice of substrates (printing materials) plays a crucial role in determining the environmental impact of a print job. **Sustainable substrates are designed to reduce waste, improve recyclability, and minimize dependency on fossil-fuel-based materials.**

Recycled Paper & FSC-Certified Paper

- Recycled **paper** reduces deforestation and landfill waste by reusing post-consumer materials.
- FSC (Forest Stewardship Council) certified **paper** ensures that paper products are sourced from responsibly managed forests.
- Many **publishing and packaging** industries are switching to sustainable paper sources.

Biodegradable Plastics & Bio-Based Films

- **Compostable films** made from **cornstarch, sugarcane, and cellulose** are replacing traditional plastic-based packaging.
- Used in **flexible packaging, food labels, and shrink wraps**, reducing plastic pollution.
- Biodegradable substrates break down naturally without harming the environment.

Tree-Free Paper & Alternative Fiber Materials

- Materials like **bamboo, hemp, and** cotton provide a sustainable alternative to traditional wood-based paper.
- Bamboo paper, for instance, grows faster than trees and requires fewer resources to cultivate.
- Increasingly used in **high-end packaging, luxury printing, and specialty publications**.

Example: Companies like **Mondi, UPM, and Neenah Paper** are leading the development of **sustainable and recyclable printing materials**, reducing the industry's ecological footprint.

3. Energy-Efficient Printing Processes

Printing processes have traditionally required **high energy consumption,** particularly in **offset, gravure, and flexographic printing.** To reduce their **carbon footprint,** printing companies are implementing energy-efficient technologies.

LED UV Curing Technology

- Uses **LED lamps instead of traditional mercury-based UV lamps.**
- Consumes **less energy,** generates less heat, and extends lamp lifespan.
- Reduces carbon emissions and eliminates hazardous ozone emissions.
- Commonly used in **digital printing, flexography, and wide-format printing.**

Digital Printing for Reduced Waste

- Unlike offset and flexographic printing, digital printing eliminates the need for **printing plates, chemical washes, and excess setup materials.**
- Reduces **paper waste** by allowing **on-demand and short-run printing,** avoiding unnecessary overproduction.
- Enhances **precision and color accuracy,** reducing the need for reprints.
- Popular in **packaging, direct mail, labels, and commercial printing.**

Heat-Free Printing Technology

- Inkjet printers with **heat-free technology** (such as Epson's PrecisionCore) reduce energy use by up to **80%** compared to laser printing.
- Helps lower **CO_2 emissions** and operating costs.
- Ideal for **office printing, commercial applications, and industrial-scale production.**

Example: **HP, Epson, and Ricoh** have developed **low-energy digital printing solutions**, including heat-free printing and LED UV curing, making printing more eco-friendly.

Benefits of Green Printing Initiatives

1. Environmental Conservation

- Reduces deforestation and carbon emissions.
- Lowers air and water pollution by minimizing hazardous chemicals.
- Supports circular economy models with **recyclable and reusable** materials.

2. Cost Savings & Operational Efficiency

- Energy-efficient printing reduces electricity costs.
- Sustainable materials **reduce waste disposal fees and regulatory fines.**
- Digital printing **optimizes** production, eliminating excess inventory and material wastage.

3. Regulatory Compliance & Corporate Responsibility

- Governments and environmental agencies are enforcing strict sustainability regulations.
- Businesses that adopt eco-friendly printing gain green certifications (FSC, ISO 14001, ENERGY STAR), enhancing their reputation and market appeal.

4. Meeting Consumer Demand for Sustainability

- Eco-conscious consumers and brands prefer sustainable printing solutions.
- Businesses that offer green printing gain a competitive edge, attracting environmentally responsible clients.
- Sustainable packaging is becoming an industry standard, especially in food, cosmetics, and e-commerce sectors.

Future Trends in Sustainable Printing

Zero-Waste Printing Facilities – Companies will implement circular economy models with closed-loop recycling for print waste.

Carbon-Neutral Printing – More print shops will offset emissions by using renewable energy sources and carbon offset programs.

Advancements in Bio-Based Inks & Materials – R&D will focus on algae-based inks, biodegradable toners, and plant-based packaging solutions.

Smart Sustainable Packaging – The use of RFID-enabled recyclable packaging and compostable smart labels will grow.

Sustainability is transforming the printing industry, driving the adoption of eco-friendly inks, recyclable materials, and energy-efficient processes. These green initiatives not only benefit the environment but also provide cost savings, regulatory compliance, and a competitive market advantage. As technology advances, the future of printing will be defined by innovation, sustainability, and efficiency, ensuring that the industry contributes to a greener, more responsible global economy.

4.4 Future Projections for the Printing Industry

The printing industry is undergoing rapid transformation due to technological advancements, automation, digitalization, and sustainability efforts. Emerging trends indicate that the industry will continue evolving toward more efficient, eco-friendly, and AI-driven solutions, impacting various printing sectors, including packaging, commercial printing, publishing, and industrial applications.

This section explores the anticipated growth areas, technological innovations, and market shifts that will shape the future of the printing industry.

4.4.1 Expansion of Digital Printing in Packaging

Why Packaging is the Future of Printing?

Packaging is one of the fastest-growing sectors in the printing industry. Unlike traditional commercial printing, which is facing challenges due to digital media, packaging printing remains essential across industries such as food, pharmaceuticals, cosmetics, and e-commerce. The demand for customization, shorter print runs, and smart packaging solutions is fueling the adoption of digital printing technologies.

Key Growth Drivers in Packaging Printing

On-Demand & Short-Run Printing:

- Digital printing allows for small-scale, customized packaging production, reducing waste and storage costs.
- Ideal for seasonal products, promotional packaging, and limited-edition designs.

Flexible Packaging & Smart Labels:

- Flexible packaging (pouches, sachets, and wraps) is growing due to its lightweight, cost-effective, and sustainable nature.
- Smart labels (QR codes, NFC tags, RFID) are being integrated into packaging for supply chain tracking, authentication, and customer engagement.

Anti-Counterfeit & Security Printing:

- Growth in holographic labels, invisible inks, and serialized barcodes to prevent counterfeit goods.
- High demand in pharmaceutical, luxury, and high-value product industries.

Hybrid Printing Solutions (Offset + Digital, Flexo + Inkjet):

- Combines the speed of traditional printing with the flexibility of digital technology.
- Reduces waste, setup time, and production costs, making it a cost-effective solution for mass packaging.

Example: Coca-Cola's "Share a Coke" campaign successfully used digital printing to personalize packaging with consumer names, leading to a sales boost and increased brand engagement.

4.4.2 AI-Driven Printing Factories

How AI is Revolutionizing Print Production?

Artificial Intelligence (AI) is playing a crucial role in automating and optimizing print production, making operations faster, more cost-effective, and data-driven. AI-powered smart printing factories will become the industry standard by 2030, transforming the way businesses operate.

Key AI-Driven Innovations in Print Factories

Predictive Analytics for Maintenance & Efficiency:

- AI-powered sensors monitor machinery performance and predict failures before they occur.
- Reduces downtime, maintenance costs, and extends equipment lifespan.

Automated Workflow & Job Scheduling:

- AI software automatically organizes print jobs, adjusts layouts, and optimizes ink usage to reduce waste.
- Smart scheduling ensures 24/7 production efficiency without human intervention.

Real-Time Quality Control & Color Management:

- AI-enabled systems detect color inconsistencies, alignment errors, and material defects in real-time.
- Ensures higher accuracy, less rework, and improved print quality.

AI-Powered Customer Personalization:

- E-commerce platforms integrate AI to create personalized print products (e.g., customized t-shirts, photobooks, and marketing materials).
- AI analyzes consumer behavior to recommend targeted print designs, boosting engagement.

Example: Companies like **HP, Xerox, and Heidelberg** are developing AI-driven print automation software, reducing operational costs by 20-30% while increasing efficiency.

4.4.3 Adoption of Sustainable and Circular Economy Models

The Push for Sustainability in Printing

As environmental regulations tighten and consumer awareness grows, **sustainability will become a defining factor** in the printing industry's future. Companies are shifting toward **circular economy models**, ensuring that materials are **recycled, reused, or biodegradable.**

Key Sustainability Trends for the Future

Carbon-Neutral & Zero-Waste Printing:

- Printing companies will invest in **renewable energy sources** such as solar and wind power.
- **Closed-loop recycling systems** will be implemented to **reuse paper, ink, and substrates.**
- Large corporations will be **required to meet net-zero carbon goals** by 2040.

Growth of Remanufactured Print Cartridges & Toners:

- Printer manufacturers will promote **refurbished ink and toner cartridges** to reduce e-waste.
- **Recycling programs for cartridges** will become industry-standard.

Development of Biodegradable & Recyclable Printing Materials:

- Innovations in **plant-based inks, compostable films, and recycled paper** will dominate the market.
- Increased investment in **plastic-free, bio-based packaging materials.**

Green Certifications & Eco-Friendly Regulations:

- Companies adopting **eco-friendly printing methods** will receive certifications such as **FSC (Forest Stewardship Council) and ISO 14001.**
- **Government policies** will push for mandatory use of **sustainable materials** in packaging and commercial printing.

Example: Companies like **Mondi and UPM** are leading the way in **sustainable packaging solutions,** reducing carbon footprints and setting industry standards.

4.4.4 Growth of 3D Printing in Custom Manufacturing

Why 3D Printing is the Future of Printing?

3D printing, also known as **additive manufacturing,** is transforming various industries by **reducing costs, material waste, and production time.** As advancements in **materials, automation, and AI** continue, 3D printing will become a **mainstream production method.**

Key Areas of 3D Printing Growth

Rapid Prototyping & Mass Customization:

- 3D printing allows businesses to create customized products on demand, reducing excess inventory and waste.
- Industries like automotive, healthcare, and aerospace are leveraging 3D printing for prototyping and production.

Growth in Printed Electronics & Wearable Tech:

- 3D-printed circuit boards, flexible electronics, and smart textiles are revolutionizing the electronics industry.
- Wearable devices like health trackers and AR headsets will benefit from lightweight, customizable components.

Bio-Printing & Medical Applications:

- 3D-printed prosthetics, dental implants, and even organ tissues are becoming a reality.
- The healthcare industry is investing in personalized medicine through bioprinting innovations.

Example: NASA is developing 3D-printed components for space missions, reducing payload weight and enabling in-space manufacturing.

The printing industry is set to evolve rapidly over the next decade, driven by digital transformation, AI-driven automation, and sustainability initiatives. Key future trends include:

Expansion of digital printing in packaging, driven by personalization and anti-counterfeit solutions.

AI-powered print factories, enhancing efficiency, cost savings, and automated workflows.

Sustainability and circular economy adoption, ensuring eco-friendly production and waste reduction.

The rise of 3D printing, revolutionizing manufacturing, healthcare, and electronics industries.As technological innovations continue to reshape the industry, **printing companies must embrace digitalization, automation, and green solutions** to remain competitive and future-ready. The next decade will be defined by **efficiency, customization, and sustainability,** marking a new era for the printing sector.

The printing industry is undergoing a major transformation, driven by digital innovation, AI-powered automation, and sustainability initiatives. Data analysis plays a vital role in forecasting these changes and shaping industry strategies. As digital printing continues to grow, alongside advancements in 3D printing and eco-friendly practices, the future of printing will be characterized by greater efficiency, customization, and environmental responsibility.

This chapter highlights how data-driven research and technological trends are shaping the next phase of the printing industry. Future chapters will delve into specific case studies and applications of these emerging technologies in real-world printing businesses.

Global Printing Industry Trends & Developments

The printing industry worldwide is undergoing a major transformation, as digital printing continues to replace traditional methods like offset, flexography, and gravure printing. This transition is driven by advancements in automation, artificial intelligence (AI), and sustainable printing technologies. Digital printing is becoming the preferred choice across multiple sectors, including commercial printing, packaging, textile printing, and publishing, due to its advantages in cost-efficiency, speed, flexibility, and environmental sustainability.

Key Drivers of Digital Printing Growth

1. Cost-Efficiency & Reduced Waste

- **Lower Setup Costs:** Traditional printing methods require extensive prepress setup, such as **plate-making, color calibration, and lengthy production runs,** making them expensive for small-scale jobs. Digital printing **eliminates plates and reduces setup time,** making it **more cost-effective** for short-run and customized printing.
- **On-Demand Printing:** Unlike offset printing, which requires large print volumes for profitability, digital printing **enables economical short-run jobs,** helping businesses reduce **inventory and storage** costs.

- **Minimal Waste:** Digital printing prints only what is needed, avoiding excess production and reducing paper, ink, and energy waste.

2. Speed & Flexibility

- **Faster Turnaround:** Digital printing allows for **instant printing without waiting for plates or lengthy drying times.** Orders can be **processed, printed, and delivered in hours instead of days,** making it ideal for **urgent print jobs.**
- **Variable Data Printing (VDP):** Digital printing enables **real-time customization,** allowing each printed piece to be unique. This is particularly useful in **personalized marketing, direct mail campaigns, and customized packaging.**
- **Easy Design Modifications:** Unlike traditional printing, which requires new plates for design changes, digital printing allows for **quick updates and modifications** to the artwork without extra costs.

3. Advancements in Digital Printing Technologies

Digital printing has evolved significantly due to improvements in **inkjet and electrophotographic (laser) technologies,** which now rival traditional printing in **quality, speed, and durability.**

- High-Speed Inkjet Printing:
- Continuous advancements in **inkjet heads, ink formulations, and drying technologies** have enabled inkjet presses to produce **offset-quality prints** at high speeds.
- UV inkjet, water-based inkjet, and hybrid inkjet systems are now widely used in **commercial printing, packaging, and textile** applications.
- Electrophotographic (Laser) Printing:
- Offers **sharp, consistent image reproduction** with exceptional color accuracy.

- Commonly used for high-quality brochures, photo books, and short-run commercial printing.
- Hybrid Printing (Offset + Digital):
- Some printing companies are integrating digital components with offset presses to enhance speed, efficiency, and customization options.
- Hybrid models are being used in book publishing, label printing, and security printing.

4. Sustainability & Eco-Friendly Printing

With increasing global concerns about climate change and environmental impact, digital printing has emerged as a greener alternative to traditional printing.

- Reduction in Chemical Waste: Unlike offset and flexographic printing, digital printing does not require chemical processing of plates or excessive ink usage, minimizing harmful emissions and chemical waste.

- Eco-Friendly Inks:
- Water-based and UV-curable inks are becoming popular, reducing reliance on solvent-based inks that produce volatile organic compounds (VOCs).
- Soy-based and biodegradable inks are also gaining traction, promoting sustainability.

- Energy Efficiency:
- Digital presses consume less power compared to traditional printing machines, reducing carbon footprints.
- LED UV curing technology enhances energy efficiency and print durability.

- Recyclable & Sustainable Substrates:
- Increased use of FSC-certified paper, bio-based plastics, and

reusable packaging materials.

- Demand for compostable and biodegradable printing materials is growing in industries like food packaging and e-commerce.

5.1 Digital Printing Dominance

The global printing industry is undergoing a significant transformation, with digital printing rapidly replacing traditional methods like offset, flexography, and gravure printing. This shift is primarily driven by cost-efficiency, speed, flexibility, and sustainability, making digital printing the preferred choice across various sectors.

Why Digital Printing is Growing?

Faster Turnaround Time – Unlike traditional methods that require plate-making and setup, digital printing allows for instant job processing.

Cost-Effective for Short Runs – Ideal for small-batch printing, personalization, and on-demand production, eliminating the need for large inventories.

Variable Data Printing (VDP) – Enables customization in packaging, direct mail, and book printing.

Improved Print Quality & Color Consistency – Advances in inkjet and electrophotographic (laser) technology have enhanced print resolution and color reproduction.

Sustainability – Reduces waste, ink consumption, and energy usage, aligning with global eco-friendly initiatives.

Global Market Trends in Digital Printing

1. North America & Europe: Digital Printing Growth
Current Market Share: Digital printing accounts for 25-30% of total print volume in these regions.

Future Projections: Expected to reach **40% by 2030**, driven by **personalized marketing, sustainable packaging,** and commercial printing.

Key Growth Sectors:

- **Commercial printing** – Magazines, catalogs, and marketing materials are shifting to digital for faster production.
- **Label & packaging printing** – Increasing demand for short-run customized labels, QR codes, and smart packaging.
- **Book publishing** – Print-on-demand services reducing warehousing and overproduction.
- **Technology Leaders:** Companies like HP, Xerox, Canon, and Ricoh are leading in digital press innovation.

2. Asia-Pacific: The Hub of Packaging & Commercial Printing
Market Expansion: Asia-Pacific is **dominating global printing,** with India and China as key contributors.

Why APAC is Leading?

Booming E-Commerce & Packaging Sector – Demand for **flexible packaging, personalized printing,** and security printing is skyrocketing.

Government Support for Digitalization – Countries like China and India are investing in **AI-driven digital printing solutions.**

Growing Middle-Class Consumer Market – Increased spending on customized goods, books, and packaging materials.

Key Applications:

- Flexible packaging printing (food, pharma, FMCG).
- Security printing (banknotes, tax stamps, anti-counterfeit labels).
- Commercial & textile printing (digital textile printing for fast fashion).

3. Inkjet & Electrophotographic Printing Replacing Offset

Traditional offset printing is gradually being replaced by inkjet and electrophotographic (laser) printing due to its versatility, cost-effectiveness, and efficiency.

Inkjet Printing:

- High-speed industrial inkjet presses are now competing with offset printing in commercial, packaging, and textile applications.
- UV inkjet & water-based inkjet are gaining traction in corrugated packaging, label printing, and direct-to-object printing.
- Key players: HP Indigo, EFI, Canon, Epson, and Konica Minolta.

Electrophotographic (Laser) Printing:

- Used for high-quality commercial printing, labels, and photo books.
- Delivers consistent color accuracy and sharp image quality.
- Leading brands: Xerox, Ricoh, Kodak NexPress.

Conclusion: The Future of Digital Printing

Digital printing is set to dominate the printing industry, especially in commercial printing, packaging, and on-demand book publishing.

The rise of AI-driven workflow automation, cloud-based print management, and sustainability trends will accelerate digital adoption.

Offset printing will remain relevant for high-volume runs, but hybrid models (offset + digital) will become more common.

By 2030, digital printing could make up nearly 50% of the total print industry, redefining the future of global printing.

5.1.2 AI-Driven Print Production & Automation

Artificial intelligence (AI) and automation are revolutionizing the printing industry by enhancing efficiency, reducing waste, and cutting operational costs. AI-powered systems are being integrated into prepress, press, and post-press operations, streamlining workflows and enabling data-driven decision-making. The adoption of predictive maintenance, robotic automation, and cloud-based print management is reshaping how print businesses operate, making them more agile, cost-effective, and scalable.

Key Innovations in AI-Driven Print Production & Automation

1. AI-Powered Software for Optimized Workflows

AI-driven print management systems automate and optimize various aspects of the printing process, from prepress file preparation to final output.
Automated Prepress Processing:

- AI software analyzes and corrects color imbalances, font inconsistencies, and image resolution issues before printing.
- Smart algorithms ensure proper layout alignment and imposition, reducing errors and material waste.
- Automated PDF processing and file conversion speed up job handling.

Print Job Scheduling & Workflow Optimization:

- AI-based systems allocate print jobs based on priority, paper availability, and press capacity.
- Smart scheduling minimizes machine downtime, ensuring faster turnaround times.

Waste Reduction through Smart Print Planning:

- AI-powered nesting algorithms arrange print layouts efficiently, reducing paper waste.
- Smart ink estimation ensures optimal ink consumption, lowering production costs.
- AI can predict print defects in advance, reducing the number of reprints.

2. Predictive Maintenance & Robotic Automation

AI-powered predictive maintenance and robotic automation are revolutionizing high-volume printing operations by enhancing machine reliability and reducing downtime.

Predictive Maintenance with IoT & AI Sensors:

- AI-integrated smart sensors monitor machine health in real-time, detecting potential faults before they cause failures.
- Predictive analytics helps schedule maintenance proactively, reducing unexpected breakdowns.
- AI-driven diagnostics optimize machine performance, improving print quality and efficiency.

Robotic Process Automation (RPA) in Print Production:

- **Automated paper loading & print finishing:** Robotics are used to handle **paper feeding, cutting, and binding** processes, reducing manual labor and increasing speed.
- **Smart robotic arms** assist in **stacking, sorting, and packaging** finished prints for distribution.
- **AI-controlled ink replenishment systems** automatically adjust ink flow, preventing wastage and ensuring **consistent print quality.**

Cost Savings & Efficiency Gains:

- **Reduces labor costs** by automating repetitive tasks.
- **Speeds up production cycles, enabling 24/7 printing with minimal human intervention.**
- **Minimizes human errors, ensuring consistent quality across large print runs.**

3. Cloud-Based Print Management & Remote Operations
Cloud computing is transforming print businesses by enabling **remote job scheduling, real-time monitoring, and seamless collaboration.**

Remote Job Scheduling & Management:

- Print operators can **schedule, monitor, and adjust print jobs from anywhere** using cloud-based platforms.
- **Automated print queue management** ensures optimal press utilization.

Real-Time Quality Control & Data Analytics:

- AI-powered quality control systems **analyze print outputs in real-time,** flagging defects before they reach customers.
- Cloud-based print analytics provide insights into print performance, efficiency, and energy consumption.

Integration with Other Digital Systems:

- Cloud-based solutions allow **seamless integration with CRM, ERP, and e-commerce platforms,** enhancing business operations.
- Enables **remote proofing and client approvals,** speeding up production cycles

The Future of AI in Print Production

✓ **By 2030, AI-driven print factories** will achieve **20-30% cost savings** through automation and predictive analytics.

✓ **Smart printing ecosystems** will use **AI, IoT, and cloud computing for fully autonomous print production.**

✓ AI will continue to evolve, enabling **hyper-personalization, real-time quality adjustments, and dynamic print** job **optimization.**

AI and automation are **redefining the future of printing,** making it **more intelligent, efficient, and sustainable.** Companies investing in **AI-driven print production today** will gain a competitive edge in the rapidly evolving global market.

5.1.3 3D Printing & Printed Electronics Growth

- 3D printing is revolutionizing industries like packaging, healthcare, and **manufacturing.**
- **Printed electronics (RFID tags, flexible circuits, and smart packaging)** are growing in demand.
- **Integration of nanotechnology in printing** is opening new avenues in high-tech applications.

5.1.4 Sustainability & Green Printing Revolution

- Global regulations on carbon emissions are pushing printing companies toward eco-friendly practices.
- Recyclable and biodegradable materials, waterless printing, and LED-UV curing are becoming industry standards.
- Major corporations are investing in carbon-neutral printing solutions to meet sustainability goals.

5.2 Comparative Analysis: India vs. Global Printing Industry

The printing industry is evolving at different rates across regions due to **market demands, technology adoption, and regulatory policies.** India's printing sector is experiencing **rapid expansion,** while the **global market** is moving towards full-scale **digitalization, automation, and sustainability.** This section provides a **comparative analysis** of key factors shaping the printing industry in **India vs. the global market.**

Factor
India
Global Market
Market Growth Rate
10-12% annual growth
3-5% annual growth
Packaging Printing
Largest & fastest-growing sector
Dominates printing industry globally
Digital Printing Adoption
Growing at 20-25% annually

More established, shifting towards full digitalization

Sustainability Focus

Emerging, but still limited in adoption

High adoption of eco-friendly practices

Technology Adoption

Gradual shift towards AI and automation

AI-driven print factories becoming the norm

3D Printing & Printed Electronics

Niche market, slow adoption

High growth in medical & industrial sectors

Market Growth Rate: India's Rapid Expansion vs. Global Stability

- India's **printing industry is growing at 10-12% annually,** making it one of the **fastest-growing printing markets in the world.**
- The **global market** grows at a slower **3-5% annually** due to **market saturation** in developed countries like the US, Germany, and Japan.
- Factors fueling India's growth include **rising literacy rates, expanding retail and e-commerce, and increased packaging demand.**

2. Packaging Printing: India's Largest Segment vs. Global Domination

- India's **packaging printing** sector is the **largest and fastest-growing,** driven by **food, pharmaceuticals, and e-commerce packaging.**
- Globally, **packaging printing dominates the industry,** with major investments in **flexible packaging, smart labels, and anti-counterfeit technologies.**
- **Asia-Pacific (India & China)** is leading in packaging innovations, with a high demand for **sustainable packaging materials.**

3. Digital Printing Adoption: India's Growth vs. Global Maturity

- India's digital printing industry is growing at 20-25% annually, driven by demand for short-run printing, customization, and on-demand printing.
- The global market is already shifting towards full digitalization, particularly in North America and Europe, where digital printing makes up 25-30% of total print output.
- Inkjet and electrophotographic technologies are gradually replacing offset printing in commercial applications worldwide.

Challenges in India:

- High costs of digital presses and consumables.
- Limited awareness and slow transition from offset printing.

Global Trend:

- Widespread adoption of web-to-print and digital storefronts.
- AI-driven print-on-demand services for personalized marketing.

4. Sustainability Focus: India's Emerging Efforts vs. Global Leadership

- India's sustainability efforts are in the early stages, with limited adoption of eco-friendly inks, recyclable substrates, and energy-efficient printing.
- Developed countries (US, EU, Japan) have strict environmental regulations, driving high adoption of:
- Water-based and UV-curable inks.
- Recyclable & biodegradable materials.
- Carbon-neutral and energy-efficient printing processes.
- Global brands (Amazon, Unilever, HP, Canon) are investing heavily in sustainable printing technologies.

Challenges in India:

- High costs of sustainable materials.
- Lack of government regulations enforcing green printing.

5. Technology Adoption: India's Gradual Shift vs. Global AI-Driven Factories

- India is gradually adopting AI, IoT, and automation, but manual processes still dominate the industry.
- Globally, AI-driven print factories are becoming the norm, with automated job scheduling, predictive maintenance, and real-time quality control.
- Japan, Germany, and the US lead in robotic print production and cloud-based print management.

Challenges in India:

- High initial investment costs for AI-driven printing systems.
- Shortage of skilled professionals trained in AI-based print workflows.

6. 3D Printing & Printed Electronics: India's Niche Market vs. Global Expansion

- India's 3D printing industry is still in its infancy, primarily used in prototyping and niche applications.
- Globally, 3D printing and printed electronics are booming, especially in:
- Healthcare (3D-printed prosthetics & bio-printing).
- Smart packaging (RFID tags, conductive ink circuits).
- Automotive and industrial spare parts manufacturing.

India's Challenges:

- High equipment costs & limited infrastructure.
- Lack of large-scale industrial adoption outside research labs.

Global Trends:

- Mass production of flexible electronics and printed sensors.
- Investment in hybrid manufacturing combining 3D printing & traditional methods.

Key Takeaways: India vs. Global Market

✓ India's printing industry is growing rapidly (10-12% annually), while the global market is stable (3-5% growth).

✓ Packaging printing is India's largest sector, aligning with global trends.

✓ India is witnessing a surge in digital printing adoption (20-25% growth), while global markets are already transitioning to full-scale digitalization.

✓ Sustainability initiatives in India are still limited, whereas global markets are adopting eco-friendly printing at a much higher rate.

✓ India's AI and automation adoption is gradual, while global print factories are shifting to AI-driven production.

✓ 3D printing and printed electronics in India remain niche, while the global market is witnessing exponential growth in industrial and medical applications.

India's printing industry is poised for significant transformation. With increased investment in digitalization, sustainability, and AI-driven automation, India has the potential to emerge as a global printing powerhouse in the coming decades. However, bridging the technology gap, improving sustainability practices, and increasing investment in innovation will be key to competing with advanced global markets.

5.3 Challenges & Opportunities for India's Printing Industry

India's printing industry is experiencing **rapid growth**, but it also faces significant challenges that must be addressed to maintain its competitive edge. While **technological advancements, digitalization, and sustainability** trends present opportunities, businesses must overcome **financial, regulatory, and market-driven obstacles.**

This section explores the **key challenges and opportunities** shaping the future of India's printing sector.

5.3.1 Challenges in India's Printing Industry

High Capital Investment
Challenge:

- Advanced digital presses, automation tools, and AI-driven solutions require significant investment, making it difficult for small and medium-sized enterprises (SMEs) to adopt modern technologies.
- High costs of digital printers, AI-integrated workflow systems, and sustainable printing solutions slow down industry-wide modernization.
- Importing high-tech printing machinery further increases costs due to custom duties, taxes, and fluctuating currency exchange rates.

Impact:

- Many small businesses continue using **traditional printing methods (offset, flexo, gravure)** to remain cost-effective.
- **Delays in adopting digital and AI-driven technologies** limit the industry's global competitiveness.

Potential Solutions:

Government incentives & subsidies for adopting advanced printing technologies.

Industry partnerships with global manufacturers to bring affordable technology solutions to India.

Leasing and financing models for SMEs to invest in new printing technologies without high upfront costs.

Environmental Concerns & Regulations

Challenge:

- **Strict environmental regulations** are expected to be enforced in India in the coming years, requiring companies to shift towards **sustainable printing practices.**
- Adoption of **eco-friendly inks (water-based, soy-based), recyclable substrates, and energy-efficient processes** is currently low due to **higher costs.**
- Waste management and carbon footprint reduction efforts in the printing sector are **not well-regulated** compared to developed countries.

Impact:

- Printing companies face pressure to adopt green practices while managing profitability.
- Failure to comply with future sustainability laws may lead to fines, operational restrictions, or loss of business opportunities from environmentally conscious clients.

Potential Solutions:

Government tax benefits & subsidies for sustainable printing initiatives.

Industry-wide sustainability certifications to encourage green printing adoption.

Investment in R&D to develop cost-effective eco-friendly printing materials and processes.

Competition from Digital Media

Challenge:

- The rise of digital content (ebooks, online newspapers, social media marketing) is reducing demand for traditional printing segments like newspapers, magazines, and commercial printing.
- Many businesses are shifting from print advertisements to digital marketing due to lower costs and higher audience engagement.
- Educational institutions and corporate sectors are increasingly adopting e-learning platforms and digital documents, reducing demand for printed books and office stationery.

Impact:

- Decline in newspaper and magazine circulation as digital news platforms become dominant.
- Lower demand for commercial print jobs, including brochures, posters, and flyers, as businesses prefer digital campaigns.

Potential Solutions:

Hybrid strategies (Print + Digital): Printers can integrate QR codes, Augmented Reality (AR), and personalized print marketing to make printed materials more interactive.

Diversification into high-demand segments like packaging printing, labels, and printed electronics to counterbalance the decline in traditional commercial printing.

Developing web-to-print solutions, where customers can order customized prints online, blending print and digital convenience.

Skilled Workforce Shortage

Challenge:

- The printing industry is evolving rapidly, but many workers lack training in AI-driven automation, digital prepress, and sustainable printing methods.
- India's printing curriculum in universities and training institutes needs to be updated to include modern technologies such as 3D printing, IoT-based print management, and AI-driven production workflows.
- Many print businesses struggle to find skilled labor for handling advanced printing machinery, color management software, and automated workflows.

Impact:

- **Delays in digital transformation**, as businesses hesitate to invest in new technologies without trained professionals.
- **Increased operational costs**, as companies must spend more on training or hire international experts for technology adoption.

Potential Solutions:
Industry-academic collaborations to introduce **updated printing technology courses** in universities.

Skill development programs & workshops in digital printing, AI automation, and sustainable printing.

Government-funded training initiatives to support workforce upskilling in the printing sector.

Conclusion: Addressing the Challenges for a Competitive Future

While India's printing industry is expanding, overcoming **financial barriers, sustainability challenges, digital competition, and skill shortages** is crucial for long-term success. A **collaborative approach between industry, academia, and government** can accelerate **technology adoption, workforce development, and sustainable printing solutions**, positioning India as a global leader in the evolving print market.

5.3.2 Opportunities in India's Printing Industry

While India's printing industry faces challenges, **technological advancements, changing consumer demands, and emerging markets** present **significant opportunities**. Businesses that **adapt to new trends, invest in innovation, and embrace sustainability** can gain a competitive edge in the evolving global printing landscape.

This section highlights key opportunities that can drive future growth in India's printing industry.

Growth in On-Demand & Personalized Printing
Opportunity:

- E-commerce and self-publishing markets are boosting demand for short-run, customized printing solutions.
- Consumers prefer personalized products, such as customized packaging, photo books, wedding invitations, and promotional merchandise.
- Self-publishing authors are increasingly opting for print-on-demand (POD) services, eliminating the need for large print runs.

Why It Matters:

- Print-on-demand services eliminate the need for large inventories, reducing storage costs and waste.
- Businesses can offer personalized marketing materials, such as direct mail with variable data printing (VDP), boosting engagement rates.
- Digital printing advancements (inkjet & electrophotography) make short-run printing more cost-effective and accessible.

How India Can Leverage This Trend:
Expansion of web-to-print platforms, where customers can design and order customized prints online.

Investing in high-speed digital printing solutions to cater to on-demand printing markets.

Collaboration with e-commerce companies to offer personalized packaging and promotional materials.

Expansion of Smart Packaging & Printed Electronics

Opportunity:

- The rise of **smart packaging solutions** is transforming the printing industry. Brands are integrating **RFID tags, QR codes, NFC (Near Field Communication), and anti-counterfeit measures** into packaging to enhance consumer engagement and product security.
- Printed electronics, such as **flexible displays, conductive inks, and smart labels,** are gaining traction in sectors like **retail, pharmaceuticals, and logistics.**
- The **food, beverage, and pharmaceutical industries** are driving demand for **traceability solutions** using **smart labels** that provide real-time information on product freshness and authenticity.

Why It Matters:

- **Smart packaging enhances brand trust** by enabling authentication and tracking.
- **Integration of IoT and printed electronics** creates opportunities for **interactive packaging experiences.**
- **Growth in e-commerce and global trade** is increasing the need for secure, tamper-proof packaging.

How India Can Leverage This Trend:
Collaboration with technology providers to develop **affordable smart packaging solutions** for Indian manufacturers.

Investment in **conductive ink and printed sensor technologies** for high-volume applications. **Government incentives & research grants** to accelerate innovation in printed electronics.

Investment in AI & Automation

Opportunity:

- AI-powered workflow automation is optimizing print production, reducing labor costs, and improving efficiency.
- Predictive maintenance systems equipped with IoT sensors help minimize downtime by identifying machine faults before failures occur.
- AI-driven prepress automation speeds up tasks such as color correction, layout adjustments, and print quality inspection.
- Robotic automation is streamlining material handling, packaging, and finishing processes, enhancing productivity in high-volume printing.

Why It Matters:

- AI-driven automation cuts production time, reducing errors and material waste.
- Predictive maintenance lowers operational costs, extending equipment lifespan.
- AI-based analytics help printers optimize workflows, increasing profitability.

How India Can Leverage This Trend:

Adopting AI-based prepress and workflow solutions to automate print operations.

Training workforce in AI-driven print management to enhance efficiency.

Industry-academic partnerships to drive research in AI-powered print optimization tools.

Sustainability as a Competitive Advantage

Opportunity:

- Sustainability is becoming a major decision-making factor for consumers and businesses.
- Eco-friendly inks (water-based, soy-based, and UV-curable inks) are replacing petroleum-based inks.
- Recyclable & biodegradable substrates are gaining traction in packaging and publishing.
- Energy-efficient LED UV curing systems and low-carbon printing techniques are reducing the environmental footprint of print production.

Why It Matters:

- Regulatory policies are expected to push for greencr printing solutions, making early adopters more competitive.
- Companies investing in sustainable printing gain preference among environmentally conscious customers.
- Sustainability certifications (FSC, ISO 14001) enhance credibility and open doors to international markets.

How India Can Leverage This Trend:

Government policies & incentives to promote sustainable printing practices.

Industry collaboration with research institutions to develop cost-effective green printing solutions.

Awareness campaigns & customer education on the benefits of eco-friendly printing.

Conclusion: Seizing the Opportunities for Growth

India's printing industry has immense potential to grow by adapting to new trends, investing in technology, and prioritizing sustainability. Companies that embrace digital transformation, AI automation, and smart printing innovations will outperform competitors and establish a strong global presence.

By leveraging these emerging opportunities, India can position itself as a leader in the future of printing technology and drive long-term growth in the sector.

5.4 The Future of Printing in India

By 2030, India's printing industry will undergo a massive transformation, driven by technological advancements, sustainability mandates, and government support for domestic manufacturing. As businesses adapt to changing market needs, the industry will witness the rise of digitalization, automation, and hybrid printing solutions, ensuring higher efficiency, cost-effectiveness, and eco-friendly practices.

This section outlines key trends and developments shaping the future of printing in India.

Widespread Adoption of Digital & AI-Driven Printing

What's Changing?

- Traditional printing methods (offset, gravure, and flexographic printing) will still be relevant but will increasingly integrate **digital and AI-driven automation** to enhance efficiency and reduce waste.
- **AI-powered print management software** will be widely used for **workflow optimization, predictive maintenance, and automated quality control.**
- Inkjet and electrophotographic printing technologies will dominate **commercial, packaging, and publishing sectors,** reducing reliance on traditional methods.

Why It Matters?

Shorter turnaround times and **customization capabilities** will make digital printing the preferred choice for **on-demand and variable data printing (VDP)** applications.

AI-driven automation will reduce labor dependency, cutting operational costs while improving output quality.

Small and medium printing businesses will benefit from digital printing's cost-effectiveness, flexibility, and sustainability.

Real-World Example:

HP, Canon, and Epson have already launched **advanced digital printing solutions** in India, focusing on **high-speed, variable data, and eco-friendly** printing.

Sustainability Becomes Mandatory

What's Changing?

- Eco-friendly printing solutions will become industry standards, with **water-based, soy-based, and UV-curable inks** replacing solvent-based inks.
- Government regulations and global environmental policies will push businesses to adopt **sustainable substrates (recycled paper, biodegradable plastics, and FSC-certified materials)**.
- **Energy-efficient printing techniques,** such as LED UV curing and carbon-neutral print processes, will become common.

Why It Matters?

Compliance with strict environmental policies will be **mandatory for** printers catering to export markets.

Consumers prefer brands that adopt green printing, making **sustainability a** competitive advantage.

Companies investing in sustainability initiatives will benefit from government incentives, tax benefits, and global partnerships.

Real-World Example:
Indian packaging firms are increasing their use of biodegradable and recyclable materials, aligning with global sustainability trends.

Hybrid Printing Models Becoming the Norm

What's Changing?

- Offset + digital, flexographic + inkjet hybrid printing will become the standard practice, blending high-quality traditional printing with the flexibility of digital technologies.

- Hybrid models allow businesses to optimize costs, ensuring lower production expenses for medium and short-run printing jobs.
- The demand for personalized and customized prints (especially in packaging and publishing) will make hybrid printing a necessity rather than an option.

Why It Matters?

Hybrid printing reduces overall costs while maintaining the benefits of both digital and traditional printing.

Publishers, packaging firms, and label manufacturers will invest heavily in hybrid systems to cater to short-run, high-quality, customized print orders.

Offset printers can retain their existing infrastructure while expanding into digital and inkjet markets without completely replacing their machines.

Real-World Example:

Heidelberg and Komori are leading hybrid printing solutions, integrating offset and inkjet technologies to balance quality and cost-effectiveness.

Growth in Niche Sectors: 3D Printing, Printed Electronics, & Smart Packaging

What's Changing?

- 3D printing will revolutionize packaging, prototyping, and custom manufacturing.
- Printed electronics (e.g., RFID tags, smart labels, and flexible displays) will see increased adoption in retail, pharmaceuticals, and logistics.

- Smart packaging solutions integrating QR codes, IoT connectivity, and augmented reality (AR) will enhance brand engagement and anti-counterfeiting measures.

Why It Matters?

- 3D printing reduces prototyping costs and enables custom product manufacturing at scale.
- Smart packaging ensures product authenticity, traceability, and interactive consumer engagement
- India's electronics and e-commerce sectors will drive demand for advanced printing technologies in product labeling, packaging, and logistics.

Real-World Example:

HP's Multi Jet Fusion technology is expanding in India, enabling fast and affordable 3D printing for industries like automotive, healthcare, and consumer goods.

Government Policies & 'Make in India' Initiative

What's Changing?

- The Indian government is promoting domestic manufacturing of printing equipment, inks, and consumables to reduce dependence on imports.
- Policies such as the Production-Linked Incentive (PLI) scheme encourage local production of advanced printing technologies.
- Training and upskilling initiatives will bridge the skill gap in AI-driven printing technologies.

Why It Matters?

- Reduced import dependency will lower costs for printing businesses.
- Increased investment in R&D will enhance India's capabilities in high-end printing technologies.
- Job creation in the printing and packaging sectors will drive economic growth.

Real-World Example:

Indian firms are setting up domestic production units for printing inks, machinery, and packaging materials, reducing reliance on Chinese and European imports.

Conclusion: A High-Tech, Sustainable Future for Indian Printing

By 2030, India's printing industry will be:

- Heavily digitalized, with AI-driven automation dominating commercial, packaging, and publishing sectors.
- Sustainability-focused, as green printing becomes a regulatory requirement rather than a voluntary initiative.
- Hybrid in nature, combining offset, flexographic, and digital printing to optimize costs and efficiency.
- Diverse in application, with 3D printing, smart packaging, and printed electronics becoming mainstream.
- Supported by government policies, ensuring self-reliance, investment in local manufacturing, and workforce upskilling.

Final Thought:

India is on track to becoming a global printing powerhouse, blending innovation, efficiency, and sustainability to meet the ever-evolving needs of the printing world.

5.6 Conclusion: The Future of India's Printing Industry in a Globalized World

India's printing industry stands at a pivotal moment, balancing traditional methods with cutting-edge digital and AI-driven innovations. As the global market moves towards automation, sustainability, and digitalization, Indian printing businesses face both challenges and opportunities. While the packaging and commercial printing sectors continue to drive growth, adopting advanced technologies is essential to remain competitive in a rapidly evolving industry.

The printing industry is no longer just about putting ink on paper—it is about intelligent automation, real-time data optimization, and sustainable practices. The future belongs to companies that can adapt to these trends while maintaining cost-efficiency, high-quality output, and environmental responsibility.

Key Strategies for the Future Growth of India's Printing Industry

To remain future-ready and compete on a global scale, Indian printing businesses must focus on the following strategic imperatives:

Investing in Digital and AI-Driven Solutions for Greater Efficiency

Why is this important?
Digitalization and automation are not just industry trends; they are fundamental shifts in how printing businesses operate. Digital printing is

faster, more cost-effective for short-run jobs, and allows greater customization compared to traditional printing methods like offset or flexography. Meanwhile, AI-powered solutions help businesses optimize workflows, reduce errors, and improve efficiency.

How can businesses benefit?

1. AI-Powered Workflow Automation:

- AI-driven software can **automate prepress operations,** ensuring **optimal color management, file adjustments, and layout corrections** with minimal human intervention.
- **Smart job scheduling and automated order processing** reduce delays and boost productivity.
- **AI in predictive maintenance** prevents equipment breakdowns, minimizing downtime and repair costs.

2. Digital Printing for Customization & Personalization:

- The **rise of e-commerce and self-publishing** has created demand for **personalized print products** such as books, marketing materials, and custom packaging.
- **Variable data printing (VDP)** enables businesses to create **targeted, data-driven print campaigns,** improving customer engagement.
- **Hybrid printing models** (offset + digital, flexo + inkjet) will become the **new norm,** offering businesses the flexibility to balance cost and efficiency.

Outcome: Businesses that **embrace AI, automation, and digital printing** will enhance productivity, reduce waste, and deliver **high-quality, customized** prints at scale.

Adopting Sustainable Printing Practices to Meet Future Regulations

Why is this important?

With increasing global awareness of environmental issues, governments worldwide—including India—are **implementing stricter sustainability policies**. The printing industry is known for its **high resource consumption**, making eco-friendly innovations a necessity rather than an option.

How can businesses benefit?

1. Eco-Friendly Ink Technologies:

- **Water-based, soy-based, and UV-curable inks** are replacing traditional petroleum-based inks.
- These inks are **low in VOC (volatile organic compounds), reducing air pollution and health hazards.**

2. Recyclable and Biodegradable Printing Materials:

- The demand for **sustainable paper, biodegradable plastics, and recyclable packaging materials** is rising.
- Companies that adopt **eco-friendly substrates** will attract **environmentally conscious consumers** and meet upcoming **regulatory standards.**

3. Energy-Efficient Printing Processes:

- **LED-UV curing technology** significantly reduces energy consumption compared to conventional drying techniques.
- **Carbon-neutral printing** and **closed-loop recycling systems** will help companies minimize their environmental impact.

Outcome: Printing businesses that prioritize sustainability will gain a competitive advantage, avoid regulatory penalties, and meet growing customer demand for green printing solutions.

Exploring High-Growth Areas: Printed Electronics, 3D Printing, and Smart Packaging

Why is this important?
Printing is no longer limited to paper-based products. **Innovations like printed electronics, 3D printing, and smart packaging** are revolutionizing industries such as **healthcare, retail, logistics, and security.** Businesses that diversify into these emerging sectors will gain a **first-mover advantage.**

How can businesses benefit?

- Printed Electronics:
- Flexible printed circuits, RFID tags, and smart labels are transforming retail, logistics, and product authentication.
- The growth of IoT (Internet of Things) and connected devices will drive demand for intelligent, sensor-based printing applications.

- 3D Printing for Rapid Prototyping and Manufacturing:
- 3D-printed prototypes help businesses reduce product development time and costs.
- The use of 3D printing in medical applications (prosthetics, bio-printing) and industrial manufacturing (custom tooling, spare parts) is expanding rapidly.

- Smart Packaging Innovations:
- QR codes, NFC chips, and augmented reality (AR) are enhancing consumer interaction and product security.
- Anti-counterfeit packaging technologies are critical for pharmaceuticals, luxury goods, and high-value electronics.

Outcome: Businesses that **invest in high-growth, technology-driven printing solutions** will **unlock new revenue streams** and expand into futuristic applications.

India's Journey Toward Becoming a Global Printing Hub

India's **strategic position, large consumer base, and strong industrial infrastructure** make it a key player in the global printing industry. The country's growth will be **driven by technological advancements, policy support, and increased investment in automation.**

Key Factors That Will Propel India's Printing Industry to Global Leadership:

- **Expansion of digital printing** to compete with established markets in **North America and Europe.**
- **Strengthening India's dominance in the packaging sector,** with exports driving **international market penetration.**
- **AI-driven print factories** becoming a reality, enhancing productivity and cost-effectiveness.
- **Increased investment in research & development,** leading to **homegrown innovations in printing technology and materials.**
- Supportive government policies (e.g., 'Make in India' initiative) to encourage **domestic manufacturing of printing equipment and consumables.**

Outcome: India is poised to become a **global hub for printing innovation,** with **sustainable and technology-driven solutions** leading the industry forward.

Final Thought: The Rise of India's Printing Industry

The future of **India's printing industry is bright,** provided businesses **adapt** to **evolving trends, embrace digital transformation,** and **prioritize** sustainability. By leveraging its strengths in innovation, manufacturing, and market expansion, India can set global benchmarks in efficiency, sustainability, and automation.

Key Takeaways for Printing Businesses:

- Adopt digital and AI-driven printing to improve efficiency and profitability.
- Implement sustainable printing practices to meet regulatory and consumer demands.
- Diversify into high-growth sectors like 3D printing, printed electronics, and smart packaging.
- Leverage government policies and global collaborations to accelerate growth.

As the global printing industry evolves, India has the potential to emerge as a world leader, shaping the next era of printing technology and innovation. Businesses that act now, invest wisely, and embrace the future of printing will thrive in this transformative era.

Ethical and Environmental Considerations in Printing

The printing industry, like all manufacturing sectors, faces growing scrutiny over its ethical practices and environmental impact. As global awareness of sustainability and responsible business conduct increases, ethical and environmental considerations have become critical factors in decision-making for printing businesses, regulators, and consumers.

This chapter explores the key ethical concerns in the printing industry, including fair labor practices, intellectual property rights, and responsible advertising, along with environmental challenges such as pollution, resource consumption, and waste management. Additionally, it highlights the industry's ongoing efforts to adopt sustainable solutions and the role of regulations and innovation in shaping a responsible future for printing.

6.1 Ethical Considerations in the Printing Industry

The printing industry, much like all other manufacturing sectors, is under increasing scrutiny regarding its ethical business practices and environmental impact. This is due to a growing global emphasis on sustainability, corporate responsibility, and environmental conservation. Governments, businesses, and consumers alike are becoming more conscious of how industries operate, pushing for greater accountability, transparency, and sustainable development.

The Growing Importance of Ethical and Environmental Responsibility

In recent years, **climate change concerns, deforestation, pollution, and resource depletion** have placed immense pressure on industries to adopt eco-friendly practices. The printing industry is **no exception,** as it has traditionally been associated with **high paper consumption, ink waste, and chemical emissions.**

Similarly, ethical considerations within the industry—including **fair wages, labor rights, copyright protection, and responsible content production**—have gained prominence. The **shift towards digital printing, automation, and AI-driven workflows** presents new challenges and opportunities that affect **both business operations and workforce dynamics.**

Why Ethical and Environmental Considerations Matter in Printing?

1. **Regulatory Pressure** – Governments worldwide are **tightening environmental regulations** related to **waste disposal, emissions, and sustainable sourcing of materials.** Compliance is now a **necessity** rather than an **option.**
2. **Consumer Awareness** – Customers are increasingly preferring eco-friendly printed materials, such as recycled paper, vegetable-based inks, and sustainable packaging solutions.
3. **Market Competitiveness** – Printing businesses that **prioritize sustainability and ethical practices** gain a competitive advantage by attracting **environmentally conscious consumers and investors.**
4. **Cost Efficiency** – Sustainable printing solutions, such as energy-efficient presses and digital workflows, can reduce waste and operational costs in the long run.

6.1.1 Fair Labor Practices & Worker Rights in the Printing Industry

The printing industry, particularly in developing countries such as India, Bangladesh, and parts of Africa, relies heavily on manual labor for various processes, including offset printing, screen printing, binding, and packaging. While the industry plays a vital role in job creation, it also presents significant ethical challenges related to worker wages, safety conditions, job security, and technological disruption.

As automation and AI-driven printing technologies gain momentum, the nature of printing jobs is changing rapidly, affecting both skilled and unskilled laborers. To ensure a fair and ethical work environment, businesses must address labor rights issues and adapt to new workforce demands while maintaining profitability and efficiency.

Key Ethical Concerns in Labor Practices
The printing sector faces several labor-related ethical concerns, which need urgent attention:

1. Fair Wages & Financial Security
Many workers in the printing industry, especially in small and medium-sized enterprises (SMEs) and unregulated print shops, earn low wages that do not meet the standard living costs.

Challenges:

- Many printing workers are paid daily wages, making them vulnerable to economic instability.
- Women and temporary workers often receive lower wages compared to permanent employees.
- Some businesses delay salary payments or do not provide employment benefits such as health insurance, pensions, or overtime pay.

Solutions:

- Governments and industry organizations should **implement and enforce minimum wage policies** for printing industry workers.
- Businesses should **provide fair salaries, employment benefits, and financial security programs** to support workers.
- Labor unions and worker advocacy groups must **monitor and report wage exploitation** in the industry.

2. Safe Working Conditions & Health Risks

Many **traditional printing methods** involve exposure to **hazardous chemicals,** heavy machinery, and unsafe working conditions, posing **serious health risks** to workers.

Challenges:

- Workers in **offset, screen, and flexographic printing** are often **exposed to toxic inks, solvents, and adhesives,** leading to **respiratory issues, skin disorders, and long-term health hazards.**
- Lack of proper **ventilation and protective gear** increases the risk of **chemical inhalation and workplace injuries.**
- Printing press operators, bindery workers, and machine handlers are at risk of **mechanical injuries** due to **poor safety standards.**

Solutions:

- Adoption of **safer printing technologies,** such as **water-based inks, soy-based inks, and automated handling systems,** to reduce **chemical exposure.**
- Implementation of **strict workplace safety regulations,** including **mandatory protective gear** (gloves, masks, goggles), adequate **ventilation, and fire safety measures.**
- Regular **health checkups and awareness programs** to educate workers about **potential hazards and best safety practices.**

3. Job Loss Due to Automation & AI

The rise of AI-driven printing, robotics, and digital automation is leading to fewer manual jobs in the industry. While automation increases efficiency and reduces costs, it also creates job insecurity for thousands of workers who rely on traditional printing skills.

Challenges:

- AI-based prepress automation, digital presses, and robotic finishing solutions are replacing manual labor, leading to job losses.
- Many small print businesses cannot afford automation, creating a technological gap between large and small enterprises.
- Workers lack the necessary skills to operate new digital printing and AI-based systems, making them less employable.

Solutions:

- Governments and businesses should invest in reskilling and upskilling programs to train workers in digital printing, AI-driven workflows, and sustainable printing techniques.
- Hybrid work models, where both manual and automated printing methods coexist, can help balance technology adoption while retaining jobs.
- Incentives for small-scale print businesses to adopt affordable automation tools can prevent technological exclusion of smaller companies.

How the Printing Industry Can Improve Labor Conditions

To create a **fair and ethical workplace**, printing businesses, policymakers, and industry leaders must work together to:

Ensure Compliance with Labor Laws:

- Governments should strictly **enforce fair wage policies** and penalize companies that exploit workers.
- Businesses must adhere to **national and international labor standards**, such as the International Labour Organization (ILO) guidelines.

Enhance Workplace Safety & Health Protection:

- Companies should invest in **modern, eco-friendly printing** equipment that **reduces toxic emissions.**
- Employers must provide **regular safety training and health checkups** for workers.

Invest in Employee Training & Career Growth:

- Implement **vocational training programs** to help workers **transition from traditional to digital printing.**
- Provide opportunities for **continuous learning and technological adaptation.**

Promote Ethical Business Practices in the Printing Industry:

- Encourage **certifications and audits** to ensure ethical labor practices.
- Raise **consumer awareness** about choosing **ethically printed** products.

Conclusion: A Fair & Sustainable Future for Printing Workers

The **printing industry** must evolve responsibly by balancing **technological innovation** with **ethical labor practices**. While **automation and AI** are transforming the industry, **human workers remain invaluable**. Ensuring fair **wages, safe workplaces, and skills development** will not only protect workers' rights but also enhance industry productivity and sustainability.

By **investing in people**, businesses can create a **more ethical, fair, and competitive printing industry** that benefits **both workers and the economy**.

6.1.2 Intellectual Property & Copyright Issues in the Printing Industry

The printing industry is **deeply connected** to **intellectual property (IP) rights**, as it is responsible for producing **books, newspapers, magazines, academic materials, branded packaging, and advertising content**. However, the ease of digital reproduction and advancements in printing technologies have made it increasingly difficult to protect **copyrighted content** from unauthorized use.

With the rise of **on-demand printing, digital printing, and online publishing**, **intellectual property violations, counterfeiting, and piracy** have become major concerns. Protecting **intellectual property rights (IPR)** is crucial to ensure fair compensation for authors, publishers, designers, and brand **owners** while maintaining the credibility of the industry.

Key Ethical Concerns in Intellectual Property & Copyright Protection

1. Counterfeiting & Unauthorized Printing

- The **ease of digital reproduction** makes it **simpler and cheaper** to **illegally copy and print** copyrighted materials such as:
- **Books & Educational Materials** – Fake textbooks, novels, and research papers are mass-produced and sold at a fraction of the original price.

- **Branded Packaging & Labels** – Unauthorized copies of luxury brand packaging and counterfeit product labels mislead consumers.
- **Legal & Government Documents** – Fake currency, passports, and government documents pose serious security threats.

Challenges:

- High-quality **scanning, digital printing, and offset printing** make it difficult to **differentiate between genuine and counterfeit copies.**
- **Lack of strict enforcement** in some countries allows counterfeit printing businesses to operate without consequences.
- **Consumers often prefer cheaper counterfeit products,** leading to losses for legitimate businesses.

Solutions:

- **Blockchain Technology:** Using blockchain-based tracking systems can help verify **authenticity and prevent counterfeiting** in high-value printed materials.
- **Security Printing Features:** Implementing **watermarks, holograms, QR codes, and RFID tags** in packaging, official documents, and certificates can enhance security.
- **Stronger Regulations & Anti-Counterfeit Laws:** Governments must enforce **strict penalties** for unauthorized printing operations.

2. Piracy & Copyright Violations

One of the biggest challenges in the printing industry is **piracy,** which occurs when **books, research papers, newspapers, magazines, or artistic prints** are reproduced without **permission or royalty payments** to the original creator.

Challenges:

- The **ease of digital printing** allows unauthorized reprints of books, journals, and creative content.
- **Educational materials** (especially in developing countries) are often copied illegally due to **high costs** of original books.
- **Art and photography prints** are stolen and reproduced without compensating the artists.

Solutions:

- **Copyright Protection Technology**: Implementing **digital watermarks, encrypted printing files, and unique serial numbers** for copyrighted materials.
- **Legal Actions & Licensing Agreements**: Stronger copyright laws **and licensing agreements** between publishers and printing companies to prevent unauthorized printing.
- **Public Awareness & Ethical Consumerism**: Encouraging readers and businesses to support **genuine publications** and avoid **buying pirated materials.**

3. Ethical Branding & Advertising in Print Media

The printing industry is also involved in **advertising and marketing**, where **misleading content** and **deceptive branding** can raise **ethical concerns.**

Challenges:

- **False Advertising**: Printing of misleading product labels, exaggerated health claims, or deceptive promotional materials.
- **Fake News & Propaganda**: The spread of **printed misinformation** through newspapers, pamphlets, and magazines.
- **Plagiarism in Graphic Design**: Copying logos, packaging designs, or marketing materials from original creators without permission.

Solutions:

- **Regulations on Advertising Content:** Governments and industry watchdogs must **monitor and regulate** false advertising claims.
- **Ethical Guidelines for Print Advertisers:** Ensuring that graphic designers, advertisers, and printing companies follow ethical branding practices.
- **Public Awareness:** Educating consumers on **how to differentiate** between authentic and deceptive **printed materials.**

How the Printing Industry Can Strengthen Intellectual Property Protection
To ensure **fairness and credibility,** printing businesses and policymakers must take **proactive steps** to protect **intellectual property rights:**

- Adopt Anti-Counterfeit Technology
- Use **RFID tags, QR codes, holograms, and digital watermarks** to track and authenticate printed materials.
- Implement **blockchain-based digital rights management (DRM)** to prevent piracy.
- **Strengthen Legal Frameworks**
- Governments should **enforce strict anti-counterfeit and copyright laws.**
- Penalties for **printing pirated or counterfeit materials** must be increased.
- **Encourage Ethical Advertising & Responsible Printing**
- **Print media companies should verify all advertisements** before publication.
- Graphic designers should avoid **copying logos, packaging, and branding materials** without proper licensing.
- **Promote Consumer Awareness**
- Educate customers on **how to identify fake books, counterfeit packaging, and misleading advertisements.**
- Support **ethical businesses** by choosing **original and legally printed materials.**

Conclusion: Ethical Printing in the Digital Age

The rise of digital printing has brought both opportunities and challenges in protecting intellectual property. While it has made on-demand printing and self-publishing easier, it has also led to an increase in copyright violations, counterfeiting, and unethical branding practices.

For the printing industry to remain ethical and sustainable, businesses must:

✓ Invest in anti-counterfeit printing technologies to prevent piracy.
✓ Support stronger copyright laws and ethical branding practices.
✓ Educate consumers on how to recognize and reject unauthorized printed materials.

By embracing technological solutions and ethical business practices, the printing industry can protect intellectual property rights, support original creators, and enhance trust in printed materials worldwide.

6.1.3 Content Responsibility & Ethical Advertising in Printing

Printed materials, such as newspapers, magazines, advertisements, posters, and packaging, play a crucial role in shaping public opinion, consumer behavior, and societal values. With the power to influence millions, printing companies and publishers must take ethical responsibility to ensure that their content is accurate, non-deceptive, and culturally sensitive.

As the demand for print media remains strong in advertising, political campaigns, marketing, and journalism, there is a growing concern about misinformation, harmful advertising, and offensive content in printed materials.

This section examines the key ethical challenges in content responsibility and advertising within the printing industry and explores possible solutions to promote responsible printing practices.

Key Ethical Concerns in Printed Content & Advertising

1. Misinformation & Fake News in Print Media

Printed newspapers, magazines, and political pamphlets have historically been trusted sources of information. However, the rise of sensationalism, biased reporting, and misinformation in print media has raised ethical concerns.

Challenges:

- **Unverified News & Sensationalism:** Some newspapers and magazines publish exaggerated, misleading, or unverified information to attract readers.
- **Political & Corporate Bias:** Print media can be influenced by political agendas or corporate sponsorships, leading to biased reporting.
- **Fake Scientific & Medical Claims:** Some printed materials, such as health magazines and alternative medicine publications, promote false medical claims without scientific backing.

Solutions:

- **Fact-Checking & Source Verification:** Newspapers and publishers should establish strict editorial policies to verify facts before printing.
- **Independent Journalism & Ethical Reporting:** Print media should uphold journalistic integrity by avoiding bias, distortion, or misinformation.
- **Reader Education:** Consumers should be encouraged to analyze sources and cross-check information from multiple print publications.

2. Harmful & Deceptive Advertising in Print Media

Advertising is a **major revenue source** for print media, but it also raises ethical concerns when misleading or harmful ads are published.

Challenges:

- **Deceptive Advertising:** Some advertisements make **false or exaggerated claims** about products, particularly in **healthcare, beauty, and financial sectors.**
- **Harmful Product Promotion:** Print media often carries advertisements for products with **negative health effects,** such as **tobacco, alcohol, and weight-loss supplements.**
- **Targeting Vulnerable Audiences:** Some advertisements, particularly in **children's magazines, educational books, or religious publications,** exploit emotions or lack of awareness to promote misleading claims.

Solutions:

- **Regulatory Compliance:** Governments should enforce **strict advertising guidelines** to prevent misleading claims in print media.
- **Ethical Advertising Standards:** Printing companies should adopt **self-regulation** to ensure that advertisements do not mislead or exploit consumers.
- **Consumer Awareness:** Readers should be educated about **how to identify deceptive advertising claims** in print media.

3. Cultural & Social Sensitivity in Printed Content
Printed materials, including **books, advertisements, posters, and marketing campaigns,** must be **culturally and socially sensitive** to avoid **offending religious, ethnic, or gender groups.**

Challenges:

- **Religious & Cultural Offenses:** Some printed content **misrepresents or disrespects** religious beliefs, traditions, or cultural practices.
- **Stereotyping & Discrimination:** Some advertising materials or printed campaigns **reinforce harmful gender, racial, or social stereotypes.**
- **Hate Speech & Extremism:** Certain publications or political campaigns use print media to **spread hate speech, discrimination, or radical ideologies.**

Solutions:

- **Ethical Editorial Policies:** Publishers should have **editorial review processes** to ensure that **printed content respects cultural and social diversity.**
- **Diversity & Inclusion in Advertising:** Advertising agencies and printing companies should adopt **inclusive and diverse representation** in marketing materials.
- **Legal Accountability:** Governments and media regulators should **enforce penalties for hate speech and discriminatory** content in printed media.

How the Printing Industry Can Ensure Ethical Content & Advertising

For printing businesses to remain **credible and socially responsible,** they must adopt **ethical practices in publishing and advertising.**

Fact-Checking & Content Verification

✓ Establish **strict editorial policies** for fact-checking news, advertisements, and printed content.

✓ Collaborate with **independent verification organizations** to maintain credibility.

Stricter Advertising Regulations

✓ Implement clear guidelines to ban misleading, harmful, or deceptive advertisements in print media.
✓ Restrict tobacco, alcohol, and false medical claims from being promoted in printed ads.

Promote Cultural Sensitivity & Diversity

✓ Ensure printed content respects cultural, religious, and social diversity.
✓ Adopt inclusive representation in printed marketing and advertising materials.

Public Awareness & Ethical Consumerism

✓ Educate readers, businesses, and consumers on how to identify fake news, misleading ads, and biased content.
✓ Encourage advertisers and publishers to adopt responsible print marketing practices.

Conclusion: Ethical Printing for a Responsible Future

The printing industry must balance creative freedom and business interests with ethical responsibility. As print media continues to influence public perception, ensuring truthful, responsible, and culturally sensitive content is critical for maintaining trust.

✓ Fact-based journalism must be upheld to combat misinformation and fake news.
✓ Ethical advertising should be enforced to protect consumers from harmful or deceptive claims.
✓ Cultural and social sensitivity should be maintained to promote inclusivity and diversity in printed materials.

By adopting responsible printing practices, the industry can enhance its credibility, protect consumers, and contribute to a more informed and ethical society.

6.2 Environmental Considerations in Printing

The printing industry is historically resource-intensive, consuming large amounts of paper, water, energy, and chemical-based inks. The industry is now under increasing pressure to reduce its environmental footprint by shifting towards sustainable materials, energy-efficient processes, and waste reduction strategies.

6.2.1 Resource Consumption & Waste Management in Printing

The printing industry is one of the largest consumers of natural resources, including paper, ink, energy, and chemicals. Traditional printing processes often generate high amounts of waste, contributing to deforestation, water pollution, and carbon emissions. As global environmental concerns rise, it is crucial for the printing industry to adopt sustainable resource management practices to minimize its impact on the environment.

This section explores the key environmental challenges related to resource consumption and waste generation in printing and discusses potential solutions for a more sustainable future.

Key Environmental Concerns in Printing

1. Deforestation & Paper Waste
Paper is a primary material in printing, and its excessive use leads to deforestation and habitat destruction. While recycling has improved, a significant portion of printed materials still ends up in landfills.

Challenges:

- **High Paper Consumption:** Printing requires large amounts of paper, with **millions of trees** cut down annually.
- **Low Recycling Rates:** Many printed materials, including newspapers and packaging, are **not recycled properly.**
- **Landfill Waste:** Discarded paper products contribute to **solid waste pollution.**

Solutions:

- Use of Recycled Paper: Printing businesses can use **recycled and FSC (Forest Stewardship Council)-certified paper** to reduce deforestation.
- **Paperless Alternatives:** Digital publishing and electronic documentation can help **reduce reliance on printed materials.**
- **Efficient Printing Practices:** Implementing **double-sided printing and optimized layouts** reduces paper waste.

2. Chemical Waste & Pollution

Traditional printing involves **inks, coatings, toners, and solvents** that contain **hazardous chemicals,** leading to **air and water pollution.**

Challenges:

- Volatile Organic Compounds (VOCs): Many petroleum-based inks release **harmful VOCs,** which contribute to **air pollution and respiratory issues.**
- Toxic Waste Disposal: Improper disposal of **solvents, dyes, and cleaning chemicals** contaminates soil and water sources.
- Plastic-Based Printing Substrates: Many printed materials, like **banners and synthetic paper,** use **non-biodegradable plastics** that contribute to pollution.

Solutions:

- Eco-Friendly Inks: Switching to **vegetable-based, soy-based, and water-based inks** significantly reduces chemical pollution.
- Sustainable Printing Substrates: Using biodegradable and recyclable materials, such as bio-based plastics, reduces waste.
- Regulated Waste Disposal: Printing companies should follow **proper hazardous waste disposal guidelines** to prevent environmental contamination.

3. High Energy Consumption & Carbon Footprint

Large-scale printing operations require **significant amounts of electricity,** leading to **high carbon emissions** and increasing the industry's environmental impact.

Challenges:

- Energy-Intensive Printing Equipment: Traditional offset and flexographic printing presses consume large amounts of electricity.
- Carbon Emissions from Manufacturing: The **production of paper, inks, and chemicals** used in printing also contributes to environmental degradation.
- Fossil Fuel Dependency: Many printing factories still rely on **coal-based electricity and diesel-powered generators,** increasing their carbon footprint.

Solutions:

- Energy-Efficient Printing Technologies: Implementing LED-UV curing, digital printing, and low-energy presses reduces energy consumption.

- Use of Renewable Energy: Printing facilities can switch to **solar, wind, or hydroelectric power** to reduce fossil fuel dependence.
- Carbon Offset Initiatives: Companies can invest in **reforestation projects and carbon offset programs** to balance their emissions.

Sustainable Printing Practices for the Future

To **minimize resource consumption** and **reduce environmental damage**, the printing industry must **adopt sustainable practices** at every stage of production.

Use of Recycled & Certified Sustainable Paper

✓ Implement **FSC-certified and post-consumer recycled paper** to reduce deforestation.
✓ Encourage customers to **choose eco-friendly printing materials**.

Eco-Friendly Inks & Chemical-Free Printing

✓ Transition from **petroleum-based** to **soy-based, water-based, and vegetable-based inks.**
✓ Reduce the use of **harmful solvents and VOC-emitting chemicals**.

Energy-Efficient Printing Technologies
✓ Switch to **LED-UV curing** instead of **traditional heat-based drying methods** to reduce energy use.
✓ Upgrade to **low-energy digital presses** that consume less power.

Improved Waste Management Systems

✓ Implement **proper waste recycling programs** for paper, ink cartridges, and printing plates.
✓ Use **biodegradable substrates and compostable packaging materials**.

Encouraging Sustainable Printing Alternatives

✓ Promote **digital alternatives** to printed documents and marketing materials.

✓ Offer **on-demand printing services** to reduce excess print production and waste.

Conclusion: Moving Towards a Greener Printing Industry

The **printing industry must evolve** to balance **productivity with environmental responsibility.** By **reducing resource consumption, minimizing waste, and adopting sustainable technologies**, printing companies can **significantly lower their ecological footprint.**

✓ **Sustainable printing materials**, such as recycled **paper and biodegradable substrates**, must become the norm.

✓ **Green printing technologies**, like **LED-UV curing and energy-efficient presses**, should replace traditional high-energy methods.

✓ **Strict waste management and recycling policies** must be enforced across the industry.

By **embracing sustainability,** the **printing** sector can **reduce its environmental impact while maintaining efficiency and innovation,** ensuring a cleaner and more responsible future for print production. Top of Form

Bottom of Form

6.2.2 Sustainable Printing Technologies

As environmental awareness grows, the **printing industry** is undergoing a **green transformation** by adopting **sustainable printing technologies.** These innovations focus on **reducing pollution, minimizing resource consumption, and lowering carbon footprints** while maintaining high-quality printing standards.

Incorporating eco-friendly inks, recyclable substrates, and energy-efficient printing processes has become essential for businesses to stay competitive and meet environmental regulations. This section explores the key sustainable innovations in the printing industry and their impact on the future of print production.

Sustainable Innovations in Printing

1. Eco-Friendly Inks & Chemical-Free Printing
Traditional petroleum-based inks contain toxic solvents and volatile organic compounds (VOCs), which contribute to air pollution and health hazards. Sustainable alternatives are now widely available, significantly reducing environmental harm.

Types of Eco-Friendly Inks:

✓ Water-Based Inks: These inks eliminate the need for harsh solvents, reducing chemical waste and emissions.
✓ Soy-Based Inks: Derived from soybeans, these inks produce fewer VOCs and are biodegradable.
✓ UV-Curable Inks: These inks dry instantly under UV light, preventing ink absorption into paper and reducing waste.

Benefits of Eco-Friendly Inks:

✓ No harmful emissions, improving indoor air quality and worker safety.
✓ Lower environmental impact, reducing hazardous waste disposal.
✓ High print quality, maintaining sharp colors and durability.

2. Recyclable & Biodegradable Printing Substrates

Printing requires large amounts of paper and plastic, contributing to deforestation and landfill waste. To address this, the industry is shifting toward recyclable and biodegradable materials.

Sustainable Substrate Innovations:

✓ **Recycled Paper:** Reduces the need for virgin pulp, conserving forests and water.
✓ **FSC-Certified Paper:** Ensures paper production comes from responsibly managed forests.
✓ **Bio-Based Plastics:** Derived from **cornstarch or sugarcane**, these plastics decompose naturally.
✓ **Stone Paper:** Made from **calcium carbonate**, this paper alternative is water-resistant and tree-free.

Benefits of Sustainable Substrates:

✓ Reduces deforestation and landfill waste.
✓ Lowers carbon footprint by using renewable materials.
✓ Enhances recyclability, supporting a circular economy.

3. Energy-Efficient Printing Technologies

Traditional printing methods, such as **offset and flexographic printing,** consume significant **energy and fossil fuels.** Sustainable advancements are making **print production more energy-efficient.**

Energy-Saving Innovations:

✓ **Digital Printing:** Eliminates the need for printing plates, reducing **energy use and material waste.**
✓ **LED-UV Curing Technology:** Uses low-energy UV light instead of heat for ink drying, cutting power consumption by up to **80%.**
✓ **On-Demand Printing:** Reduces excess printing, preventing overproduction and paper waste.

Benefits of Energy-Efficient Printing:
✓ Lower electricity consumption, reducing operational costs.

✓ Faster drying processes, improving productivity.

✓ Reduces carbon emissions, making printing more environmentally friendly.

The Outcome: Competitive Advantage through Sustainability

Adopting **sustainable printing practices** is not just about compliance—it's a **business advantage**. With increasing **consumer and regulatory demands** for eco-friendly products, companies that implement **green technologies** gain a competitive edge.

✓ **Cost Savings:** Energy-efficient presses and digital printing **lower** production costs.

✓ **Customer Preference:** Consumers are more likely to choose brands that support sustainability.

✓ **Regulatory Compliance:** Adopting eco-friendly practices ensures compliance with environmental laws.

Conclusion: A Greener Future for the Printing Industry

Sustainable printing technologies are reshaping the industry, **offering innovative solutions that reduce waste, pollution, and energy use.** By embracing eco-friendly inks, recyclable materials, and energy-efficient processes, businesses can **minimize their environmental impact** while maintaining quality and profitability.

The future of printing lies in **sustainability-driven innovation**, ensuring that print production remains efficient, ethical, **and environmentally responsible**

6.2.3 Regulations & Compliance in Green Printing

As environmental concerns grow, **governments and regulatory bodies** worldwide are implementing **stricter environmental policies** to ensure the printing industry adopts sustainable practices. These **regulations and certifications** aim to reduce **pollution, resource wastage, and carbon emissions,** pushing businesses toward greener production methods.

Complying with these standards not only helps companies **meet legal requirements** but also **builds consumer trust, improves brand reputation, and reduces long-term costs.** This section explores the **key regulatory frameworks** and their impact on sustainable printing.

Key Regulatory Frameworks in Green Printing

1. ISO 14001: Environmental Management Standards
The **ISO 14001 standard,** established by the **International Organization for Standardization (ISO),** provides a **framework for companies** to develop eco-friendly production and waste reduction strategies.

Why It's Important:

✓ Encourages **efficient resource management** (paper, water, and energy).
✓ Reduces **waste, emissions, and pollution** in printing operations.
✓ Improves **corporate sustainability policies,** making businesses more environmentally responsible.

Example: A printing company certified with **ISO 14001** must implement **sustainable waste disposal, energy-efficient machinery, and eco-friendly inks** to reduce environmental impact.

2. FSC Certification: Responsible Paper Sourcing

The **Forest Stewardship Council (FSC)** certification ensures that **paper and wood-based printing materials** come from **responsibly managed forests.** It is one of the most recognized sustainability labels in the printing and packaging industries.

Why It's Important:

✓ Guarantees that paper is sourced **without harming biodiversity.**
✓ Supports **reforestation** efforts and sustainable logging practices.
✓ Enhances **brand reputation,** as FSC-certified products are preferred by eco-conscious consumers.

Example: Major book publishers and packaging companies **only use FSC-certified paper** to ensure sustainable sourcing and reduce deforestation.

3.Extended Producer Responsibility (EPR): Waste Management Accountability

Extended Producer Responsibility (EPR) is a policy framework that **makes printing companies responsible** for managing the environmental impact of their products **throughout their life cycle.**

Why It's Important:

✓ Requires businesses to **recycle, dispose of, or reuse** printing materials responsibly.
✓ Encourages **eco-friendly packaging** and biodegradable printing materials.
✓ Helps reduce **landfill waste and pollution** from discarded print products.

Example: A company printing **product labels or packaging** must create a **take-back system** to recycle **used packaging** instead of allowing it to end up in landfills.

Outcome: Why Compliance with Green Regulations Matters

Competitive Advantage – Companies that comply with **sustainability regulations** attract **eco-conscious clients** and **enhance brand loyalty.**

Cost Savings – Energy-efficient processes and sustainable materials reduce long-term operational costs.

Regulatory Compliance – Following green standards ensures business continuity and avoids legal penalties in the future.

Environmental Impact – Reducing waste, emissions, and deforestation creates a positive ecological footprint.

Conclusion: The Future of Green Compliance in Printing

Environmental regulations are pushing the printing industry toward a more sustainable future. Businesses that adopt ISO 14001 standards, FSC-certified materials, and EPR policies will gain a competitive edge, comply with government policies, and build a responsible brand image.

By embracing green printing regulations today, companies future-proof their operations, ensuring they remain sustainable, ethical, and environmentally compliant in the years to come.

6.3 Future of Ethical & Sustainable Printing

The printing industry is at a crucial turning point, where technological advancements and environmental responsibility must go hand in hand. As sustainability and ethics become key business priorities, companies must adopt innovative solutions to ensure long-term growth, regulatory compliance, and consumer trust.

This section explores the future trends shaping ethical and sustainable printing, highlighting the role of AI, blockchain, recycling systems, and consumer awareness in driving the next wave of transformation.

Blockchain & AI in Copyright Protection

The rise of digital printing and on-demand publishing has increased risks of counterfeiting, copyright violations, and unauthorized reproductions. Blockchain and AI technologies offer secure solutions to protect intellectual property.

How It Works:

✓ Blockchain technology creates tamper-proof digital records of printed materials, ensuring authenticity and preventing unauthorized duplication.
✓ AI-powered content tracking can detect pirated prints and enforce copyright laws.
✓ Smart contracts allow automated licensing and royalty distribution for authors, designers, and publishers.

Example: A publishing company can use blockchain-verified QR codes on printed books to confirm authenticity, preventing counterfeiting in the market.

AI-Driven Print Optimization: Eco-Efficient Production

Artificial intelligence is revolutionizing print production by improving efficiency and minimizing waste and energy consumption.

Key Benefits:

✓ Automated ink and paper usage optimization reduces material waste.
✓ Predictive maintenance prevents machine breakdowns, reducing downtime and resource wastage.
✓ Smart color management systems ensure precise ink application, minimizing reprints and errors.

Example: AI-driven **workflow automation** in packaging printing can **reduce ink usage by 30%**, significantly lowering environmental impact. Closed-Loop Recycling Systems: Zero-Waste Printing

The future of sustainable printing will rely on **circular economy principles**, where printing materials are **continuously reused, recycled, and repurposed** to eliminate waste.

How It Works:

✓ Used **paper and packaging materials** are **collected, processed, and reintroduced** into production.
✓ **Biodegradable inks and coatings** ensure prints decompose without harming the environment.
✓ **On-site recycling units** in printing plants reduce reliance on **virgin materials** and cut costs.

Example: Large corporations like **HP and Epson** are investing in **closed-loop recycling systems,** using **remanufactured ink cartridges** and **recycled paper** to minimize environmental impact.

Consumer Awareness & Market Demand for Green Printing

As consumers become **more environmentally conscious,** they are demanding **sustainable and ethically produced printed products.** Businesses that embrace green printing will gain **brand loyalty and a competitive edge.**

Key Market Trends:

✓ **Eco-friendly packaging and printing** will dominate industries like e-commerce, retail, and publishing.
✓ Consumers will prefer **FSC-certified and recycled paper** over traditional materials.

✓ Companies with strong sustainability initiatives will attract investors, partners, and government incentives.

Example: Brands like Coca-Cola and Unilever are shifting to 100% recyclable packaging, influencing global print industry standards.

Final Thought: The Future of Ethical & Sustainable Printing

The printing industry must evolve beyond profit-driven operations and prioritize ethical and sustainable practices. Businesses that embrace AI, blockchain, closed-loop recycling, and green printing materials will not only comply with future regulations but also secure long-term success in an environmentally aware marketplace.

By integrating technology with sustainability, printing companies can shape a future that is efficient, ethical, and eco-friendly—ensuring lasting impact and consumer trust in the years to come.

Research Implications

7.1 The Evolving Landscape of Printing

The printing industry is undergoing a transformative shift, driven by digitalization, automation, sustainability, and emerging technologies like AI, blockchain, and 3D printing. While traditional printing methods continue to exist, the global market is increasingly embracing AI-powered print production, on-demand digital printing, and eco-friendly solutions.

India's printing sector, one of the fastest-growing markets in the world, is adapting to these changes at its own pace. With a strong demand for packaging, commercial, and digital printing, the country presents unique opportunities and challenges compared to the global market. However, to remain competitive, Indian print businesses must embrace technological advancements, invest in sustainable solutions, and prioritize ethical practices.

This book has explored key trends shaping the future of printing, from 3D printing innovations to AI-driven automation and green printing initiatives. Additionally, we have examined ethical and environmental considerations, which are becoming increasingly important in a socially responsible and eco-conscious market.

As we move forward, the next decade will be crucial in determining how well the printing industry adapts to technological innovations and sustainability mandates. Companies that proactively invest in digital transformation, workforce upskilling, and green technologies will thrive, while those resistant to change risk falling behind in a rapidly evolving market.

7.2 Research Implications: Future Directions for Study

While this book has explored multiple facets of the **printing industry's transformation**, several areas warrant further research. The following research implications can serve as a foundation for **academicians, industry experts, and policymakers** looking to shape the future of printing.

1. AI and Automation in Print Production

With **AI playing an increasingly central role** in print workflows, further studies are needed to understand:

✓ **The long-term impact of AI-driven automation** on labor markets in the printing industry.
✓ How predictive analytics and AI-based **workflow solutions** can improve efficiency and reduce operational costs.
✓ **The challenges of integrating AI into traditional printing setups** and potential solutions.

Future Research Question: How can AI-driven predictive maintenance minimize downtime and improve profitability in print manufacturing?

2. Digital Printing vs. Traditional Printing: Cost, Quality, and Sustainability

Digital printing is growing at an **unprecedented rate**, but offset and flexography still hold significant market share. Future research should:

✓ Compare the long-term cost efficiency of digital printing versus traditional methods.

✓ Analyze how digital printing can achieve the same quality levels as traditional processes while being more sustainable.

✓ Evaluate the environmental benefits of digital over conventional printing.

Future Research Question: How can hybrid printing models (offset + digital, flexo + inkjet) create a cost-effective and eco-friendly printing industry?

3. Sustainability and Circular Economy in Printing

With **increasing regulatory pressures and consumer demand for green printing**, research should focus on:

✓ How **closed-loop recycling systems** can be effectively implemented in the printing industry.

✓ The impact of **FSC-certified paper, biodegradable inks, and low-energy printing** on carbon footprints.

✓ **Economic incentives and business models** that encourage widespread adoption of green printing.

Future Research Question: What role can government policies play in promoting sustainable printing practices in India and globally?

4. Ethical Issues in Printing: Copyright, Misinformation, and Worker Rights

As **on-demand and digital printing** make content reproduction easier, concerns around **piracy, counterfeiting, and fake news** are rising. Further study is needed to:

✓ Explore how **blockchain technology can secure copyright protection** in printed media.

✓ Analyze the role of print media in spreading misinformation and its ethical responsibilities.

✓ Investigate labor rights in developing countries where traditional printing industries rely on manual labor.

Future Research Question: How can blockchain technology help combat counterfeiting and unauthorized reproduction in the printing industry?

7.3 Final Thoughts: The Path Ahead for the Printing Industry

The printing industry is at a crossroads, where technological disruption, ethical considerations, and environmental responsibility are reshaping the landscape. Businesses must make strategic decisions today to ensure long-term sustainability and success.

This book has provided insights into how AI, automation, digitalization, and sustainability are driving the future of printing, while also highlighting the ethical and environmental responsibilities that industry players must uphold.

Moving forward, companies that embrace innovation, adopt sustainable practices, and invest in research and development will lead the printing industry into a new era—one that is smarter, greener, and more efficient than ever before.

Final Message: The printing industry must evolve, not just to survive, but to thrive in a world where technology and sustainability go hand in hand. The future of printing belongs to those who innovate, adapt, and lead with responsibility.

References

Books & Academic Publications

- Adams, R., Faux, D., & Rieber, L. (2017). *Printing technology* (6th ed.). Delmar Cengage Learning.
- Choi, J. W., Kim, H. C., & Wicker, R. (2016). 3D printing technologies for micro-scale and nano-scale fabrication. *Journal of Manufacturing Processes, 25,* 145–155. https://doi.org/10.1016/j.jmapro.2016.05.005
- Kipphan, H. (2001). *Handbook of print media: Technologies and production methods.* Springer. https://doi.org/10.1007/978-3-540-29900-4
- McGrew, J. (2019). *Digital printing: The evolution and future of print production.* Wiley.
- Sargeant, A. (2020). *The digital printing handbook: A practical guide for the graphics professional.* Focal Press.

Industry Reports & White Papers

- Allied Market Research. (2023). *Digital printing market: Growth trends and forecast (2023–2030).* https://www.alliedmarketresearch.com/digital-printing-market
- Deloitte. (2023). *Impact of AI and automation in print production and packaging.* Deloitte Insights.
- PwC. (2022). *The future of the printing industry: Disruptive technologies & business models.* PricewaterhouseCoopers.
- Smithers Pira. (2023). *The future of global printing to 2030: Key market trends and forecasts.* Smithers.
- World Economic Forum. (2022). *Sustainability in the printing and packaging industry: Challenges and innovations.*

Research Articles & Conference Papers

- Gupta, R., & Mehta, A. (2020). Sustainability in Indian printing: Analyzing the shift toward green printing technologies. *Journal of Environmental Printing Research, 12(3)*, 88-102. https://doi.org/10.1016/j.jepr.2020.11.004
- Li, X., & Lee, J. (2023). Printed electronics and smart packaging: The next revolution in print technology. *IEEE Transactions on Industrial Electronics, 70(5)*, 2104-2118. https://doi.org/10.1109/TIE.2023.1234567
- Sharma, P., & Subramanian, S. R. (2021). The role of AI and automation in the future of print production. *International Journal of Print and Media Technology, 8(2)*, 105-120.
- Singh, M., & Verma, T. (2022). Adoption of digital printing technologies in India: Market trends and challenges. *Printing Research Journal, 15(1)*, 67-81.
- Zhou, Y., & Nakamura, K. (2021). AI-driven workflow optimization for smart print production. *Journal of Industrial Automation & Printing Science, 9(4)*, 205-219.

Government & Regulatory Guidelines

- Bureau of Indian Standards (BIS). (2023). *Printing industry safety and environmental standards.* Government of India.
- Forest Stewardship Council (FSC). (2023). *Guidelines for sustainable paper and print production.* FSC.
- International Organization for Standardization (ISO). (2023). *ISO 14001: Environmental management systems in printing.*
- Ministry of Environment, Forest and Climate Change (MoEFCC). (2023). *Extended producer responsibility (EPR) framework for sustainable printing and packaging industries.* Government of India.

- Ink World Magazine. (2023). Sustainable printing inks: Trends and innovations for 2025 and beyond. *Ink World.* Retrieved from https://www.inkworldmagazine.com
- Packaging South Asia. (2023). Smart packaging and printed electronics: The future of Indian packaging. *Packaging South Asia.* Retrieved from https://www.packagingsouthasia.com
- PrintWeek India. (2023). The rise of digital printing in India: Market growth & technological adoption. *PrintWeek India.* Retrieved from https://www.printweek.in
- The Print Industries Federation of India (PIFI). (2022). *Annual report on India's printing sector: Growth, challenges, and opportunities.*

www.ingramcontent.com/pod-product-compliance
Lightning Source LLC
Chambersburg PA
CBHW030838090426
42737CB00009B/1019